THE
AMBASSADOR'S
STORY

THE
AMBASSADOR'S
STORY

THE UNITED STATES
AND THE
VATICAN IN WORLD AFFAIRS

THOMAS PATRICK MELADY

Our Sunday Visitor Publishing Division
Our Sunday Visitor, Inc.
Huntington, Indiana 46750

Dedication

To the four women in my life:

My mother, Rose Belisle Melady,
my wife, Margaret Badum Melady,
and my daughters, Christina Melady Morin
and Monica Melady Micklos

Appreciation

The author wishes to express his appreciation to the Lyne and Harry Bradley Foundation, Pueblo Institute, and Freedom House for their support in the preparation of this project.

The author is also indebted to his two predecessors, Ambassadors William A. Wilson and Frank Shakespeare, for assisting him with information and events that occurred during their watch as U.S. Ambassadors to the Holy See.

Table of Contents

PREFACE

O N OUR last Sunday afternoon in Rome, Margaret and I made our farewell visit to Saint Peter's Basilica in Vatican City. In the excavations beneath the magnificent main altar, we knelt at the Tomb of Saint Peter and prayed that God would continue to inspire Pope John Paul II in his campaign for human rights and religious freedom. Leaving the crypt below, we stopped at Michelangelo's *Pietà* and were overwhelmed as always by the beauty of this masterpiece.

Since the official car was waiting for us at the rear of the Basilica, we passed two Swiss guards. I took my last salute from them as the U.S. Ambassador. Our car then proceeded over the Tiber River and east to the Trevi Fountain. We joined the laughing, joyous Romans and tourists. It was Roman sunset time. We each threw our coins into the fountain and whispered our wish — to return one day to Rome.

The following day, Monday, passed quickly with farewell calls. Finally it was Monday night, March 1, 1993, around 7:30 in the evening. Margaret and I were at the Termini, the railway station in Rome. We had been there many times during our four years in Rome, coming and going, but this was to be our last visit for some time. We were leaving Rome at the completion of my tour of duty as U.S. Ambassador to the Holy See. We had been accompanied to the train station by my immediate staff: Cameron Hume, Damian Leader, and Ted Osius. Also with us were my two drivers, Umberto and Claudio, the police escorts, and my two bodyguards, Pietro and Franco.

We chatted in pleasant banter on the train platform about our many memorable experiences in Rome. Suddenly we knew we had to say good-bye. It was difficult to hold back the tears, as we had loved Rome and everyone knew it. Finally, Cameron said lightly, "We'll be seeing you," as Margaret and I, along with Pietro and Franco, boarded the night train for Munich. We went to our compartment, inviting Pietro and Franco in to have a drink with us. We chatted some more about a few of the interesting things we had done during our stay in Rome, then embraced and said good-bye. The two bodyguards would actually accompany us all the way to the Italian-Swiss border. As the train pulled out of the station, we kept on smiling and waving. The tears came later.

My service as U.S. Ambassador to the Holy See from 1989 to 1993 was an extraordinary experience for me. My goal in this book is to share these experiences with the public, as I believe that the U.S., as the world's only superpower, and the Holy See, as the only worldwide moral-political sovereignty, have significant roles to play in the future. Their actions will impact on the lives of people in all parts of the globe.

In December 1988, when President-elect Bush told me that he wanted me to join his administration, I told my wife that the one position I wanted to receive was that of Ambassador to the Holy See. Later I mentioned it to several key members of the transition team and one member of George Bush's staff. They warned me it was not likely that I would receive that appointment. An assistant told me that there were several major contributors to consider, each having contributed at least $100,000 to the Bush-for-President campaign and/or related Republican party funds. My financial contributions, on the other hand, had consisted of several small gifts to former students at the university where I had been president. And these former students were Democrats!

When I was told in January 1989 that the President was ready to consider me for an appointment, I was also informed that I should write him a note indicating what I would like to do in his administration. Since I thought that it would be difficult to obtain the position because of the competition for the Vatican post, I indicated in my note to the President that I would like to serve in the Department of State as an Assistant Secretary. My wife was around when I wrote the note, and I showed it to her. She said to me rather sternly, "Tom, tear up the letter and indicate to the President what you really want to do." I then prepared a second note indicating that I would like to serve as the Ambassador to the Holy See.

Two days later the President phoned to offer me the position. I immediately responded: "I would be honored!" I sensed then that at this time in history the position of Ambassador to the Holy See would be important to U.S. interests. The significance of the events I was to witness during my ambassadorial assignment, however, would actually greatly surpass whatever I imagined. I will always be grateful to my wife for urging me to indicate to the President what I wanted to do, and to President Bush for giving me this opportunity to serve my country.

I had met the Pope in 1979 during his visit to New York. While it was a routine introduction, even then I had a sense that he would be a man of destiny. Born into a working-class family on the outskirts of Krakow, southern Poland, in 1920, Karol Wojtyla lived through periods of Nazi and communist oppression. An articulate spokesman for traditional values, he is very much a man of the modern world who knows how to lead and to inspire.

He was elected Pope on October 16, 1978, and I was to present my credentials to him in the eleventh year of his pontificate as Vicar of Christ, head of the Universal Catholic Church, and sovereign of Vatican City State. I was arriving in Rome as the U.S. Ambassador to the Holy See — the Government of the Catholic Church. And the Pope was the head of the Holy See.

Within a few weeks after my arrival in Rome in August 1989, it became apparent that very significant changes in the world were taking place. One superpower was disappearing; communist domination in Eastern Europe was ending, and many of the long-simmering regional conflicts in Africa, Central America, and the Middle East were being resolved. But other problems were developing in areas freed from Soviet domination. In some ways it was simultaneously the "best of times . . . the worst of times." Representing the United States at this critical moment gave me a unique opportunity to witness at first hand the convergence and parallelism of interests that frequently exist between the Holy See and the United States on the key challenges in the world during these times.

Not only geopolitical matters, but other serious worldwide concerns in health, economics, and social welfare are of profound interest to both the Holy See and the United States. For example, during my watch at the American Embassy, Pope John Paul II issued his encyclical *Centesimus Annus* on the world's economic order. Following in the footsteps of his predecessors, John Paul II set forth a broad framework of guiding principles for an economic order based on social justice for all.

Being accredited as the Ambassador to the Holy See at the end of the twentieth century is an experience very similar to the role of ambassadors to other states in the nineteenth century, when the job was less complex. My 136 colleagues during my time there represented their chiefs of state and governments. We were involved almost exclusively in diplomatic and policy matters, and we had small staffs to advise us, to report on and influence Holy See policy. Unlike embassies to major countries, we did not have staffs dedicated to military, visa, economic, trade, drug, tax, or intelligence matters. Embassies to the Holy See are classical diplomatic posts because they are concerned only with policy matters between the two governments. The mandate of the Ambassador of the United States is to represent the government of his country on matters of diplomatic and political interest to the U.S. government.

The Pope as Vicar of Christ or the religious teachings and interpretations of the Catholic Church are not within the scope of the American ambassador's assignment. Such matters as appointments of bishops, ordinations of priests, religious doctrine, anti-abortion strategy, or the ordination of women priests are not items for the ambassador of the United States to discuss with the Holy See. In this regard the U.S. Embassy is different from many other embassies. Each embassy follows the laws and traditions of its own country. We were the American embassy, where there is strict separation of church and state. For example, while some of my colleagues may have attended briefings given by the congregations of clergy and bishops or taken part in other purely religious functions, the American Embassy concentrated on the Secretariat of State in its diplomatic activities only, plus offices concerned with development, refugees, and health matters. As the U.S. Ambassador I attended all official functions called by the Holy Father. Many of them were ceremonies where Mass was the central function. In a technical sense, however, these were state functions, also attended by colleagues who were not Catholic and some who were not Christian. For me personally, these functions were also religious. When President Bush invited me to become ambassador in 1989, I studied very carefully the background to the establishment of the embassy. I knew that in 1984 there had been considerable opposition from various groups within the United States, including several Roman Catholic leaders and organizations. In the case of the Catholic groups, it was clear that they feared the ambassador would become involved in the appointment of bishops or in other matters related to the clergy or religious doctrine. I knew it was extremely important that we not only *not* become involved but that we not even give the *appearance* of being involved. I did various things to ensure this. For example, as is true with many communities the Catholic ecclesiastical leadership was divided on various issues. Some were classified as "traditional," others as "liberal," while still others had more divergent points of view. There were individual Church "politics." I made a very strict rule that no one at the embassy should become involved in these Church matters, as this was not the proper role for the Embassy of the United States.

This was also true with other religious leaders. We had a good number of leaders from the Jewish community and various Protestant churches who visited the embassy. I instructed the staff that even though the title of a "Reverend" or Rabbi might not sound as impressive as that of a Cardinal, all were Americans and all were to be treated the same. This was the Embassy of the Government of the United States and it served all Americans equally in terms of their business with the Holy See.

Only on one occasion during my almost four years as the U.S. Ambassador to the Holy See was there an attempt to have me become involved in strictly ecclesial matters, and that was a very innocent one. About six months after my arrival, a couple appeared in the office who had just arrived that morning after an overnight flight from New York City. They told me they had an envelope for me which contained confidential information on the background of a priest who they believed was a candidate for appointment as a bishop. I immediately stopped them from discussing the matter, trying to be as polite as possible. I told them I was so sorry they had traveled all this way to see me because I couldn't in any case even receive the material nor continue the conversation. I briefed them on the role of the U.S. Ambassador to the Holy See and informed them that any such proposals or information should be given to Church authorities. At no time was I ever asked by the Department of State or anyone at the White House or by any governmental official to go beyond the official scope of my mandate.

Our policy interests ranged through Vietnam, Panama, Haiti, China, the former Soviet Union, the civil strife in ex-Yugoslavia, the Gulf War, Israel, Sudan, Somalia, Liberia, and all significant developments in the world concerned with religious freedom, human rights, political pluralism, and humanitarian affairs.

I had served in the late 1960s and early 1970s as the U.S. Ambassador to Burundi and Uganda respectively. The two decades of difference between my first and second tours as ambassador were significant in that the impact of instant communications and the end of great geographic distance as far as travel is concerned brought all embassies throughout the world very close to Washington, D.C. I saw this so clearly in the case of Manuel Noriega of Panama. When the U.S. government would send me information to brief me on what was going on, it normally came after I had seen it on CNN. And when cables would come giving me instructions, it was frequently after I had already received the information by an immediate phone call from the Department of State.

There are now two U.S. Embassies in Rome: The U.S. Embassy to the Republic of Italy and The U.S. Embassy to the Holy See. There is also a U.S. Mission to the Food and Agricultural Organization of The United Nations. During my tenure as Ambassador to the Holy See, Mr. Peter F. Secchia was Ambassador to Italy. There were two Ambassadors in Rome and our missions were distinct and different. Quite simply Ambassador Secchia was the Ambassador to Italy; I to the Holy See. Both governments were located in Rome.

The American Embassy to Italy provided various administrative services (such as communications and supplies) to the American Embassy to the Holy See, and staffs might see one another at social functions in and around Rome. But their missions were separate. The relationships between the two U.S. Embassies in Rome during my tenure were very good.

I have written this overview for the general public because I believe that international public policy will benefit when the general public knows and understands the roles of the major players in world affairs. And the United States and the Holy See are, in different ways, major players in the affairs of this world.

CHAPTER I

The Opportunity for a More Just World Order

MY FIRST major assignment that involved the White House was to obtain the Pope's evaluation of Mr. Gorbachev after he met with the Pope on December 1, 1989. The White House and the Department of State knew that this was not really their first contact. There had been an evolving relationship starting in 1985 with Gorbachev. President Bush and Secretary of State Jim Baker had not yet made a judgment on Gorbachev. The essential question in the critical issues facing the United States, the United Nations, and the world: Could Gorbachev be trusted? My instructions were to report not only the details of the visit but to obtain very critical information on the judgment of the Pope concerning the character of Mikhail Gorbachev.

Rome was in beautiful splendor — lots of the traditional Roman sunshine — on December 1, 1989, when Soviet President Gorbachev and his wife, Raisa, entered the Vatican's inner court. Gorbachev, following the tradition of visiting chiefs of state, took a salute from the Swiss guards and then was introduced to the gentlemen in waiting of the papal court. Pope John Paul II, in an obviously friendly mood, received Gorbachev in his library for the private meeting, while Foreign Minister Eduard Shevardnadze and his team met with Cardinal Agostino Casaroli, then Vatican Secretary of State. The Pope campaigned for "freedom of conscience" legislation, which Gorbachev promised to support in the then Soviet Union. Freedom of religion was a major agenda item, and senior Vatican officials later told me that Gorbachev inspired confidence that he would continue on the path of assuring that freedom of religion would be a fundamental right for everyone in the Soviet Union.

Gorbachev then indicated a desire for diplomatic links with the Holy See, inviting the Pope to visit the Soviet Union. Pope John Paul responded that such matters as a visit and diplomatic links could be worked out as soon as the changes in the U.S.S.R. were more apparent. The Pontiff made a strong case for continued improvement of religious freedom and human rights.

Pope John Paul urged Gorbachev to work toward an end to confrontation between the superpowers. He congratulated Gorbachev on the changes that already had taken place and offered support to protect "the rights and duties of individuals and peoples."

The Soviet approach was a dramatic change from that of Joseph Stalin, one of Gorbachev's predecessors, who had dismissed Pope Pius XII's concerns in 1944 about establishing communist dictatorships in Eastern Europe with a sarcastic remark, "How many divisions does he have?" The 1989 meeting of Gorbachev and the Pope at Vatican City was a remarkable turn of events after forty-five years. Gorbachev had requested this meeting. He wanted the Pope to understand his plan for change in the then Soviet Union, and of course he wanted the Pope's support.

The chief question for me was the judgment of the Pope and his key aides, especially Cardinal Casaroli, about Gorbachev. Agostino Casaroli was, at age seventy-five, in his retirement year. His service to the Holy See had included over two decades of orchestrating contacts with Eastern European countries and the then Soviet Union. His early, cautious contacts in Warsaw, Budapest, Prague, and Moscow brought him considerable criticism. Some said he was too willing to compromise. He was, in fact, the architect behind the papal strategy in Eastern Europe. While giving the appearance of being very cautious, he knew when to take chances.

Now, at the end of his career, he saw his efforts come to fruition in the administration of Pope John Paul II. In the earlier years, despite criticisms that even came from high echelons within the Vatican, he continued his "step-by-step" policy of making contacts with communist government leaders. His counsel was critical through the 1988-1990 period in guiding papal strategy toward Poland and the then Soviet Union.

I had met the Cardinal before I was named ambassador. Within a few weeks of my arrival, even before presenting my credentials to the Pope, I established a firm working relationship with him. He was cooperative and forthcoming on the exchange of information and the discussion of strategy.

Cardinal Casaroli had been in contact with Gorbachev shortly after he came to power in 1985. In a meeting soon after that, Gorbachev told Cardinal Casaroli that his mother was a deaconess in the Russian Orthodox Church. Furthermore, when he visited his mother in her modest cottage, she would remove photos of Marx and Lenin from the wall, thus exposing two religious icons.

In the four years from the 1985 meeting to the 1989 rendezvous in Rome, the Rome-Moscow relationship became more friendly, with correspondence between Gorbachev and the Pope and even a Christmas greeting from Gorbachev. Several years of contacts preceded the December 1, 1989 meeting. In one of the preliminary meetings, Gorbachev referred to the spiritual influence of his mother.

We knew that the Vatican was pleased by the change they saw in Moscow. But was this change authentic? Was Gorbachev's commitment to change genuine? The Department of State and the White House were anxious to have the papal evaluation before Gorbachev would meet two days later with President Bush and Secretary of State James Baker off the island of Malta. Within hours of the Vatican meeting, I was able to report to the President and the Secretary of State that the meeting between the Pope and the Soviet leader had been a very successful one and that the Pope and his senior colleagues believed that Gorbachev was firmly committed to change in the U.S.S.R. Furthermore, it was clear — the Pope thought Gorbachev could be trusted. Needless to say, that evaluation was helpful to the President in his meeting with Gorbachev only a few hours after my report arrived off the island of Malta. This meeting between President Bush and Gorbachev, similar to the meeting of Gorbachev with the Pope, was critical in terms of establishing a climate of confidence between the Soviet and American leaders.

Both meetings were significant in terms of Pope John Paul's and President Bush's evaluation of their policies towards Gorbachev in the critical period of change that followed in the early 1990s. Gorbachev emerged within a few years of his coming to power in 1985 as a significant geopolitical orchestrator of the rapid changes then occurring in the Soviet Union. And he orchestrated the changes without any significant violence.

During those important transition years of 1989-1991, Gorbachev was trusted by both Pope John Paul II and President Bush. As the role of leadership for Gorbachev came to an end with the demise of the U.S.S.R. in the closing days of 1991, Boris Yeltsin emerged into prominence. The first appearance abroad for him in his new leadership position was on December 20-21, 1991, when he called upon Italian government officials and the Pope. Boris Yeltsin was anxious to obtain the confidence of the Pope as Gorbachev had done.

My report to the Department of State on the Yeltsin meeting was that Boris Yeltsin gave every indication that he was committed to carrying out reforms initiated by Gorbachev. He did not seem to have a plan, but his attitude was reassuring. During Yeltsin's visit, the special representative of the Soviet Union, Ambassador Jurij Karlov, became the representative of the Russian Federation. With the passing of Gorbachev from the scene, I detected a feeling of some regret among Vatican officials. The relationship with Gorbachev had evolved over six years. He was a known quantity. They trusted him.

The New Community

Yeltsin's quick dash to see the Pope on December 21, 1991, was another sign that great geographic distance had been eliminated. Only a half century ago, the oceans that separated the continents required weeks and months for travelers to go from one continent to another. The oceans, mountains, and great land masses remain, but modern transportation has drastically reduced the time it takes to travel from one formerly distant point to another. The year 2000 will see further reductions in the time required to go from one continent to another. The phenomenon of fast and easy travel has been accompanied by its relatively inexpensive nature. I flew to Rome in nine hours in August 1989 to present my credentials to Pope John Paul II. By the beginning of the new century it will be around four hours.

The end of great geographic distance has been accompanied by the phenomenon of instant communications. People in all parts of the world can be in instant contact with one another by telephone or by fax. At the Embassy I received important messages by fax within a minute after the Washington telephone call alerting me that a message was on its way.

This revolutionary change in communications has had a major effect on world affairs. We know in most cases immediately when a significant event is occurring and thus are able to do something about it. Both President Bush and the Pope knew within minutes about the attempted coup d'état in the Soviet Union in August 1991. This event, if it had been successful, would have stopped the transformation to democracy then occurring in the Soviet Union. But the quick response by world leaders like President Bush, Pope John Paul II, and British Prime Minister John

Major helped to inspire international public opinion in favor of Mikhail Gorbachev, the quarterback of change in the then Soviet Union. Gorbachev, recipient of the Nobel peace prize, led the then Soviet Union from 1985 through 1991 in a series of monumental changes that transformed what was a monolithic dictatorship into an association of republics leaning toward liberal democracy. And in the critical years of 1990 and 1991 he was supported by both President Bush and Pope John Paul II. One of my principal responsibilities was to coordinate the exchange of information and strategies on this matter between Washington and the Holy See. We did it by telephone, cable, and fax.

Examples of the important new factor of instant communications in the world geopolitical equation abound. The coverage given to the famine in Somalia, Ethiopia, and the Sudan brought this ongoing tragedy to the immediate attention of the world. The television scene of the starving child holding out his hand for a few pieces of rice was seen by millions throughout the world. And the result was an outpouring of relief supplies to assist the people there. Previously such famines were reported many months and years later in studies with statistics on what occurred. These reports were usually accurate but were too late to energize an effective response to a human tragedy. Contemporary television has changed all this, covering the tragedy while it is occurring.

The Noriega Challenge

On December 24, 1989, at 9:17 P.M., the operations center of the U.S. State Department phoned me at the residence in Rome to inform me that General Manuel Noriega, the Panamanian dictator, had entered the Vatican Nunciature in Panama City. I immediately went to the chancery to await my instructions.

I had been dressing to prepare for the midnight Mass at Saint Peter's Basilica. Since I would be seated with the diplomats, I was dressed in formal attire. Not knowing what would happen, I kept the formal attire on and rushed to the chancery, arriving there around 9:40. While waiting for a phone call from Washington, I immediately started watching the Noriega drama on CNN. The instructions eventually came over the phone. I later received a classified telegram message on what I was to do, but most of my information on the actual events was instantly communicated to me by television. I saw it, and so did the rest of the world.

My instructions were clear: The United States government did not want the Holy See to grant asylum in the nunciature to Noriega. There was a great danger that he would become a symbol for left-wing elements and anti-American groups throughout the world. This effort to capture Noriega was very important to President Bush. It was the first international operation in his anti-drug crusade.

I was urged to see Cardinal Casaroli that evening, which meant right after midnight Mass. I was told to approach him formally on behalf of the United States government. I declined to do this, as I thought it was inappropriate to request an official meeting at that time. I decided to make it personal. The midnight Mass would end at around two o'clock in the morning. Once I arrived at the midnight Mass, I sent Cardinal Casaroli a brief note indicating to him that if he had a moment I would like to speak to him informally and personally after Mass. Christmas Eve Mass was important to me. I had never missed midnight Mass. I tried to concentrate on the liturgy, but my mind wandered. I knew how important this matter was to President Bush. It was difficult to focus on the Mass because of the interruptions. As I returned to the diplomatic section after receiving Holy Communion, two Ambassadors stopped me to inquire about the latest news concerning Noriega.

Cardinal Casaroli came up after Mass, shook my hand, and told me he was aware of the fact the Noriega had been admitted to the nunciature in Panama. He too had seen it on television. Briefly I gave the Cardinal our position that Noriega was a criminal and should not be granted asylum. I indicated to Cardinal Casaroli that I would be in contact with him about a meeting on December 27. I knew December 26 was a traditional holy day for Vatican personnel and I did not want to disturb that tradition.

As I was leaving Saint Peter's Basilica, various members of the press came up to me asking for a statement. I was essentially able to avoid them for a time.

It became apparent by Christmas day that Noriega did not have many friends in the world. Both at the residence and the embassy, we began getting calls from people wanting to know why the Vatican was giving shelter to that international criminal. On December 27 I met with Archbishop Angelo Sodano, substitute secretary for relations with the states, who in fact was then the minister of foreign affairs for the Vatican. I informed Archbishop Sodano that our case against Noriega was based on his being an international drug criminal. I pointed out that an indictment had been returned against him in the federal courts of the United States many months before. It later turned out that this was a very important development.

In subsequent discussions with both Archbishop Sodano and Cardinal Casaroli, I sensed they had an appreciation of the essential fairness of the American judicial system. I therefore asked Washington for a full copy of the indictment. It was faxed to me, and I immediately delivered it to the officials at the Vatican. I had made a strong case in Vatican circles for the United States campaign against drug merchants. We had previously been in contact with Vatican officials on the growing drug menace, and we knew we had their concurrence on the seriousness of the drug problem. Following my meeting with the Pope in October 1989, there had been several strong papal statements on the drug menace.

At my presentation of credentials as the U.S. Ambassador on October 3, 1989, the Pope had said, "The profound threat to human freedom posed by the illegal traffic in narcotics is but one example [of common problems]. The curse of drug addiction, which hovers like a dark cloud over entire nations, is surely one of the most serious menaces to freedom in our time."

Along with James Creagan, the Deputy Chief of Mission, I continued to push forward our claim that Noriega was in fact an international criminal. Our sources at the Vatican told us that the drug-criminal accusation, as well as Noriega's bad record on human rights, was building an atmosphere friendly to the U.S. position. American Church leaders contacted me with reports that the Catholic Church leadership in Panama had a very low estimate of Noriega because of his long dictatorial rule that showed a contempt for human rights.

Believing that the Vatican decision would be in our favor, I nonetheless cautioned the Department of State against expecting the Holy See to respond favorably to the U.S. request in a matter of a few days. I advised that the Holy See could not give the impression of caving in to U.S. pressure. President Bush's office, Secretary of State Baker, and Undersecretary Robert Kimmit understood my evaluation, but I received several phone calls from lower-ranking staff complaining that the Vatican was taking too long. In the meantime, at the nunciature in Panama City, General Noriega was not acting like a grateful houseguest. We received rather direct reports that he had been cool and unpleasant toward

Archbishop Laboa, the nuncio who had taken him in on December 24. Noriega was known for his vehement dislike for religion and had been regarded as the most unfriendly person toward the Catholic Church in Central America for many years before this happened.

I presented the American case at some length to Archbishop Sodano, the de facto foreign minister, on December 27. The following day, December 28, I was asked to meet with Cardinal Casaroli. Jim Creagan, Deputy Chief of Mission, accompanied me. We reported to Washington that we were confident no permanent asylum would be granted to the Panamanian dictator.

Noriega was essentially given three choices by the nuncio. He could stay, but there was no guarantee that the nuncio would remain at that residence. Once the nunciature moved out, Noriega would no longer have the protection of the papal flag. The second possibility was to surrender to the Panamanian people, and the third choice was to surrender to authorities of the United States government. It was immediately apparent that he would not take the chance of surrendering to his own people, and so on January 2 he informed the nuncio that he was prepared to surrender to the American authorities providing the following arrangements were made: he asked that a clean uniform be made available to him so that he could surrender in proper attire, and that no photos be taken of the surrender; he also requested there be safe passage for his wife, children, and mistress to go to Cuba.

Archbishop Laboa was in contact with United States authorities and was thus able to guarantee this. On January 3, 1990, Manuel Noriega surrendered to U.S. authorities. Actually, I saw it first on television. It was only thirty minutes later that I was officially informed by the United States government that Noriega had surrendered.

In addition to the fact that Noriega had been indicted months before the December 1989 incident as an international drug lord, it was apparent from the period of December 24 to January 3 that the worldwide communications community had little respect for him. With the exception of the communist left-wing press, the general editorial comment on Noriega was unfavorable. Certainly in terms of telephone calls — and we had many, both at the residence and at the Embassy during this period — all but one raised basic questions about the Holy See's even considering asylum for Noriega. For these few days I defended the decision of the nuncio to give him temporary refuge until a decision on asylum could be made. During this time, I was restricted to Rome; that is, the Department of State requested that I always be there, I would frequently bump into people in restaurants or hotels — and there was a great outpouring of support for the U.S. position.

International interest in the Noriega case was an example of the impact of modern communications. Foreign policy decisions were once the prerogative of a few world leaders, and these decisions were frequently made in secrecy. Now, instant communications bring the ongoing developments to millions of people throughout the world. Consequently, international public opinion also influences world leaders. Academic, church, and legal voices can now be raised to influence these decisions. One aspect of the Noriega problem surfaced a year later at his trial in Florida. The Department of State informed me that Noriega's defense lawyers would reveal that his telephone conversations from the nunciature in Panama had been bugged. I thought it prudent to inform the Vatican immediately, so they would not be unpleasantly surprised when this would be reported in the newspapers. I arranged for my deputy to brief Monsignor Celli. He responded by saying that he was not surprised. There was very little press coverage of this disclosure.

This world community that is developing on the eve of the twenty-first century means that we are all next-door neighbors. Major geopolitical forces consequently have a unique opportunity to work together for the international common good. The United States, as the only major superpower, and the Holy See, as the government of the Catholic Church with its worldwide network, have unique strengths in moral authority that have been enhanced by the recent geopolitical changes in the world community. The 1980s saw the end of the superpower confrontation. The subsequent economic collapse of the Soviet Union left the country in a vacuum as far as fundamental values were concerned. The "atheistic" state had fought religious institutions, beliefs, values, and traditions inspired by Christian teachings.

Thus, as the "evil empire" collapsed in 1991 from internal weakness, the peoples of what had been the Soviet Union found themselves free once again to embrace political and moral values that are an intrinsic part of Judeo-Christian civilization. The collapse of a superpower was a geopolitical phenomenon. And it was a major factor in placing the United States and the Holy See in unique world roles of primordial influence for the twenty-first century.

The previous Soviet-U.S. confrontation had impeded the evolution of the world community. During the Cold War, the developing countries in Africa, Latin America, and the Middle East would frequently align themselves with either the Soviets or the Americans on various issues. Untold billions in valuable resources were committed to the armaments race. The United Nations was paralyzed by confrontations on major political problems. As senior advisor to the United States delegation to the U.N. general assembly in 1970, I had spent most of my time trying to convince African delegates to vote for the U.S. position and against the Soviet one. Since 1990 there has been frequent cooperation between the U.S. and Russia delegations at the United Nations.

Once the Soviets clearly accepted the reality of the devastating decline, Gorbachev could initiate the process of serious dialogue with the United States. Cardinal Casaroli told me that the decision of President Reagan to maximize U.S. military strength so the U.S. was superior to the Soviets was the major factor in the Soviet decline. This dialogue soon evolved into a parallelism of Soviet-U.S. interests and a unity of approach in 1989-1992 on such historic issues as Southern Africa, the Gulf War, and the Middle East.

The change in relationship between the Holy See and the Soviet Union became apparent in the visit of Gorbachev to the Pope in 1989. Coinciding with the Gorbachev visit was the opening by the Soviets of a cultural exhibit at the Vatican of one hundred icons portraying the religious heritage of the Soviet peoples. I recall seeing Mr. Gorbachev escorting the Holy Father from painting to painting and giving the background of some of them. During this time, Soviets accredited a representative to the Holy See, and the Vatican reciprocated by sending an envoy to Moscow. Once he arrived, the Soviet — later Russian — representative was one of the most active members of the diplomatic corps accredited to the Holy See.

Later, in August 1991, it was Pope John Paul II and President Bush who dramatically supported Gorbachev during the attempted overthrow of his government by a rump group that wished to reestablish the old communist dictatorship. President Bush and the Pope were joined by the leaders of France, Germany, Great Britain, and Japan. The initial support of Pope John Paul II and President Bush came within hours of the attempted coup and played a major role in energizing worldwide support at that time for Gorbachev. The quality of support for the coup that tried to stop the democratic movement can be seen by who they were: Saddam Hussein of Iraq and Muammar al-Qaddafi of Libya. The leaders of state-directed terrorism were disappointed that the attempted coup against Gorbachev had failed.

In December 1991, Boris Yeltsin, in a visit with the Pope and a telephone call to President Bush, assured both leaders that the historic changes in the old Soviet Union to democratic ideals of religious freedom, political pluralism, and human rights would be protected and continued.

On December 25, 1991, the United States and the Holy See observed, with some emotion, the demise of the Soviet Union — the end of Gorbachev's leadership and the transition to the "commonwealth" of independent states. Several months later, on March 3, 1992, Mikhail Gorbachev, the former leader of the Soviet Union, declared in an interview that Pope John Paul II had played "a major political role" in the collapse of communism in Eastern Europe.

Transforming of Authoritarian Regimes into Democratic Societies

Concomitant with the significant change in U.S.A.-U.S.S.R. relationships was a change on the world scene from authoritarian regimes to democratic governments. Dictatorships of the right, like Chile and Paraguay, and those of the left, like Nicaragua, Poland, Czechoslovakia, Hungary, and Bulgaria, evolved into governments rooted in political pluralism with guarantees for religious freedom and human rights. One-party dictatorships of Africa, like Zambia, Senegal, and Nigeria, began to recognize the dangers of one-party rule and facilitated democratic elections. The evolution to democratic governments in Africa has been slow. And there have been reverses, as with the decision of the Nigerian generals to cancel the results of their national elections in 1993.

The transformations were evolutionary. Consequently, the imperfections of the old authoritarian regimes did not disappear overnight. Some still remain. The new governments also did not become paragons of virtue vis-à-vis human rights in the early stages of the transformation. Furthermore, in the case of Eastern Europe and the Balkans, since the change from communist dominations to democracy was evolutionary, it was only natural that some communist leaders would remain in the governments — in jobs ranging from minor positions at the local level to top national positions. But change has been taking place, from authoritarian communism to leadership committed to democratic ideals at both local and national levels.

These significant changes have occurred in most parts of the world without any serious violence. The major exception to this is Yugoslavia, whose story will be discussed in Chapter IX. The commitment of the United States to a strong international campaign for human rights, commencing with the Carter administration in 1976, and the worldwide effort of Pope John Paul II and his predecessors were leading catalysts of this change. In a March 3, 1992, interview, Gorbachev said that the Pope's influence came from the political dimension of the Gospel that requires the Church to defend human rights and religious freedom. These two factors — human rights and religious freedom — have been the cornerstones in the foreign policy of Pope John Paul II.

Starting with his first trip outside of Italy on January 25, 1979, when he visited the Dominican Republic, Pope John Paul II has visited more than 120 countries. The Pope's central theme in all of these visits was to encourage a greater commitment to religious freedom and human rights. Whether in then communist-controlled Poland or the then one-party state of Zambia, his message of religious and political freedom was always the same. Equally strong was the papal emphasis on evolutionary change and the avoidance of bloodshed.

The most dramatic evolution to a government "of the people" was in the former Soviet Union. Lithuania, Latvia, and Estonia became independent. Gorbachev kept his promise to the Pope and President Bush. The Soviet Union would not impede the transfer of political power to local peoples who clearly wanted it and sought it through constitutional means.

The Lithuanians, especially, became impatient in 1990 and wanted independence that year. But both the Holy See and the United States appreciated Gorbachev's sensitive position and concurred with his opinion that the granting of independence to Lithuania and the other two Baltic states in 1990 would seriously weaken his position in Moscow. The Holy See, at our suggestion, counseled the Lithuanian leaders to give Gorbachev a little more time. The Lithuanian and other Baltic leaders did. In December 1991 the three Baltic states received their independence.

Furthermore, on Christmas Day 1991, Gorbachev followed constitutional procedure and resigned as the last leader of the defunct

Soviet Union. Russian troop withdrawal from the Baltic states had fallen behind the schedule established in 1991. Again both the Holy See and the United States were understanding about the desire of Moscow to find adequate housing for their former troops in Russia before their return to the Russian homeland.

On January first, the diplomatic corps and their families were invited to a reserved section of one of the balconies overlooking Saint Peter's Square. This was an excellent location to see and hear the Pope give his New Year's greeting and message to the world.

It was also a good place to pick up gossip. Vatican officials mixed with diplomats. The festive mood of greetings intermingled with concern about what was going on in the old Soviet Union. My report to Washington the following day reflected the concern of the Vatican about how well Yeltsin could fill the leadership vacuum caused by the departure of Gorbachev.

Concern for the transformation going on in what had been the Soviet Union was reflected in the Pope's address on January 11, 1992, to the members of the diplomatic corps accredited to the Holy See. He referred to "new structures of political cooperation" and called for the world community to "insure that the changes taking place did not occur against the backdrop of poverty." Following the meeting, I was able to speak with the Pope several minutes and briefly referred to the meeting that would take place in Washington several days later on the economic needs of the Russian people. Two days later the Holy See announced it would send a delegation to the conference called by President Bush to energize assistance to the peoples of the old Soviet Union.

There are certain unique times in world affairs. By the end of the 1980s Pope John Paul II had assured the place of the Holy See as an active and major geopolitical player in the contemporary world. The sudden and total collapse of communism in Eastern Europe and in the Soviet Union gave the Holy See a new optimism to expand its role in influencing the political and economic culture of the world.

Having been a very significant factor in the defeat of communism, the Holy See would now advocate, with strength and commitment, a worldwide acceptance by all nations of religious freedom, human rights, and political pluralism. And that advocacy converged with the overall policies of the United States supporting this trinity of human values.

CHAPTER II

New Hopes — New Problems in the 1990s

FOLLOWING a very busy end of year in December 1989 — with our success in bringing Panamanian dictator Manuel Noriega to face a trial on international drug related issues and the great success of the Gorbachev visit, first with Pope John Paul II on December 1 and then forty-eight hours later with President Bush and Secretary Baker — Margaret and I decided to spend several days in the homeland of Saint Francis of Assisi.

Saint Francis had always been my favorite saint. For me he personified love, caring for people, and true spirituality. We spent several days walking through the hills of Assisi, visiting the chapels he established in the countryside.

The chapels were all so simple. And they were surrounded by flowers and the sweeping panorama of Umbria. Following these two days of tranquillity, we returned to Rome full of enthusiasm for the new year.

The year 1990 brought much hope that the end of the superpower confrontation would open up a period in world affairs where human rights, religious freedom, and political pluralism would prevail. The administrations of the United States and the Holy See were optimistic that the world was entering a period less inclined toward dictatorships and government promotion of ethnic, religious, and social alienation.

This world situation, so full of promise in 1900, brought the policies of the United States and the Holy See closer in most areas of the world.

The United States has long been an eloquent spokesman for religious freedom, human rights, and political pluralism. Starting with the Declaration of Independence in 1776 and restating it on historic occasions like the Atlantic Charter, the U.S. has always been an advocate of this trinity of values.

The Cold War and all the other negative perceptions generated by the superpower conflict clouded the public perception of the U.S. government commitment to these rights and freedoms. With the end of the confusion caused by the Cold War, there was a general recognition of the moral authority of the United States because of its commitment to these human values.

When the United Nations, responding to worldwide pleas, established a military operation in Somalia in 1992 to assure the safe arrival of humanitarian relief supplies, it was the United States that assumed most of the burden.

The pontificate of John Paul II, starting in 1978, soon took full advantage of the worldwide network of the government of the Catholic Church to expound the moral necessity of a worldwide commitment to human rights and religious freedom.

While a strong advocate of these rights, the Holy See is less enthusiastic about the Western model of government guaranteeing political pluralism. They have not seen it work in some areas of Africa.

In addition to using speaking engagements on his trips outside of Italy, the head of the Catholic Church has a massive worldwide network, and beginning with the reign of John Paul II in 1978 the Holy See took full advantage of its world connections to advocate its position on these and other matters.

The worldwide Catholic network is divided into metropolitan dioceses and dioceses with over 400,000 clergy and about 4,200 bishops. The government of the Catholic Church consequently extends to all parts of the world. The predominant Catholic populations are in Europe and in North and South America. But the number of Catholics in Africa is growing. Less well known is the network of Catholics in the Eastern Church, going back to the early days of Christianity. The governmental network of the Catholic Church extends to these areas also where many significant political events occurred in the 1990s. Some of the most important items of information that Vatican officials shared with me came from these sources.

They include:

1. The Maronite Church, with large concentrations in Lebanon, Brazil, and Syria and over two million members around the world.
2. The Chaldean Catholic Church, with over 400,000 members in Iraq.
3. The Malabar Catholic Church, with almost three million followers, mostly in India.

4. The Armenian Catholic Church, with almost 200,000 members in Armenia, Syria, Egypt, and other countries.

5. The Coptic Catholic Church, with around 175,000 members mostly in Egypt, and the Ethiopian Catholic Church with more than 125,000 members in Ethiopia.

6. The Syrian Catholic Church, with over a 100,000 members scattered in Lebanon, Turkey, Iraq, and other countries of the Middle East.

7. The Melkite Catholic Church, with over two million members in the same countries.

The Ukrainian Catholic Church has over four million members in Ukraine. The Romanian Catholic Church in Romania and the Slovak Catholic Church are also part of the international Catholic community.

The vast worldwide network of the Catholic Church was a major reason for President Franklin Roosevelt's giving a great deal of attention to finding a way to establish diplomatic relations with the Vatican. He developed the "Personal Envoy" concept, which is discussed in Chapter III. Myron Taylor, the first U.S. Personal Envoy, found that the Vatican during World War II was a great source of strategic information for the United States.

Almost one billion Catholics are scattered over all parts of the world, including approximately 92 million in Africa, 468 million in North and South America, 290 million in Europe, and 89 million in Asia.

I knew that the Catholic community was worldwide. In preparing for my assignment in the spring of 1989, I was surprised to learn that the network extended to areas where rites other than the predominant Latin rite (that of most American and European Catholics) existed for Catholics in Eastern Europe, the Middle East, and parts of Africa.

As the Ambassador of the United States I would meet with the heads of these Catholic communities when they visited Rome. They came primarily on Church business, which they would discuss with the Pope and his senior colleagues. When they met with my staff and with me, we would discuss the important political events going on in their countries.

Cardinal Paulos Tzadua, head of the Ethiopian Catholic Church, was in Rome on several occasions during the final days of communist dictator Mengistu's reign in Ethiopia. His analysis of the Ethiopian situation, which he gave me on two different visits to Rome, was very valuable, and I promptly reported his views to Washington.

The Ethiopian rite of the Catholic Church traces its roots to the fifth century. The Popes have had a very long attachment to the Ethiopian Catholic community. A chapel was constructed very close to Saint Peter's Basilica within the walls of the Vatican in memory of a fifteenth-century visit of Ethiopian priests and bishops to Rome.

I lived in Ethiopia in 1955-1956 and attended Ethiopian Catholic liturgical services from time to time. It did not surprise me that during the brutal communist dictatorship of Mengistu, the Ethiopian Catholic Church was able to withstand the tyranny. The Church is now playing a role in the rebuilding of the country.

The Catholic Church organizations in the Ukraine and in Armenia were the source of information that led Vatican officials to sense in the early 1980s that significant changes were beginning to take place in the Soviet Union. The same Catholic network was reporting similar attitudinal changes in all of the Eastern European countries.

The value of this information, which was being shared with the office of the Personal Envoy to the Holy See, William A. Wilson, in the early 1980s, was one of the reasons influencing President Ronald Reagan to elevate the diplomatic post from a mission to a full embassy in 1984.

This mosaic of believers forms the worldwide Catholic community headed by the Pope. The Holy See is the government of this international community, and Vatican City State, in the heart of Rome, is the seat (the "See") of the Pope, Supreme Pontiff of the Catholic Church and so recognized by the United States in 1984 as a Sovereign Personality in the world community. It is this worldwide network that gives the Pope the unique ability to influence governments and peoples. It also gives the Holy See excellent sources of information.

Once diplomatic relations were established in 1984, the United States was able to collaborate with the Holy See on the exchange of information and on strategies to accomplish shared goals. One such collaboration was going on when I arrived at the embassy in 1989. The Ukrainian Catholic Church was headquartered then in Rome. James Creagan, the Deputy Chief of Mission, had an excellent relationship with the Ukrainian Church staff. We exchanged information and strategies. The Ukrainian Catholic network extended to all parts of western Ukraine. As in the Ukrainian situation, U.S. and Vatican goals normally converged during my tour of duty at the Vatican. The only significant exception was the Gulf War.

One area of divergence was on the use of force. The Holy See now gives strong emphasis to the process of nonviolent change. While once recognizing that the use of force could be justified when the cause was just, the Holy See is becoming increasingly reluctant to accept the historic "just war" theory.

The United States, on the other hand, has said that the "just war" criteria can still be justified in modern times. Moreover in 1992 when the United States undertook its effort in Somalia, the Holy See praised this military intervention because it was primarily for a humanitarian purpose. There obviously needs to be an understanding between the U.S. and the Vatican about when intervention is "just."

The United Nations: the Holy See — a Strong Supporter

Within hours of the birth of the United Nations at San Francisco in 1945, the international organization, designed to reflect a universal moral authority, was seriously crippled by major-power confrontations from action on significant political problems. Its power was restricted to non-vital issues, and even then the Cold War frequently blocked an effective U.N. response.

Forty-five years after its founding in 1945, the authoritative Security Council could act on a momentous international issue — the Gulf War brought about by Saddam Hussein's unilateral invasion of Kuwait. The major powers — not frozen by previous ideological commitments — could participate in the debate on what the world should do. The action sanctioned by the United Nations in 1990 against Iraq was witnessed by millions of people around the world on their televisions sets. This action was publicly adjudicated, and the world thus participated in the decision-making process.

The U.N. role in the Middle East crisis of 1989-1990 reinvigorated the ability of the world organization to act on behalf of a major consensus. Within a few months after this, the term of the incumbent secretary general expired, and the United Nations selected a secretary general who would have greater possibility to exercise executive authority.

Finally, almost at the end of this century and almost a half-century after its birth, the United Nations could play a more decisive role in identifying fair, just, and peaceful solutions for world problems.

The Holy See always looked positively on the role of the United

Nations. This was an area of divergence in the policies of the United States and the Holy See for a number of years. Starting with the administration of President Johnson in the 1960s and until the end of the superpower confrontation period in 1989-1990, the United States was less than enthusiastic about the role of the U.N. in world affairs.

I served as senior advisor to the U.S. Delegation to the U.N. General Assembly in 1970. This was the beginning of the period of the rising influence of Third World nations. I had one such experience with the "independent" attitude of the African leaders.

Julius K. Nyerere, then President of Tanzania, had agreed to see President Nixon on a certain day in Washington during his stay at the United Nations. He also made other appointments including a speaking engagement with a small group of Maryknoll sisters. Shortly after President Nyerere arrived in New York, Dr. Henry Kissinger, the Assistant to President Nixon, phoned to tell Nyerere that there was a schedule conflict, and the appointment had been switched to the date when he had planned to speak to the Maryknoll sisters.

President Nyerere told Dr. Kissinger that he could not change the speaking engagement. An irate aide to Dr. Kissinger phoned me and gave me instructions to call on President Nyerere and "straighten him out"; seeing the President of the United States has priority over a speaking engagement with Catholic nuns. I called on President Nyerere, who said that the Maryknoll sisters had been very helpful to the people of Tanzania and he could not change his appointment. Nyerere said to me, "I will see the President the next time."

These kinds of incidents irritated the U.S. mission and the Department of State. More important to the U.S. government was the selective attitude of the U.N. in the 1960s and 1970s, constantly criticizing the United States and Israel but ignoring human-rights abuses in the Third World.

The Holy See, on the other hand, was more patient with the U.N. volatility. In my discussions with the Vatican Mission to the U.N., the two key themes were "patience in the short term," as the concept of a worldwide authoritative body would mature and be of service to the people of the world.

The visit of Pope Paul VI to the United Nations on October 4, 1965, was intended to give support to this worldwide organization. The Holy See knows the value of a worldwide network with a central authority guided by universal principles. Another visit intended to manifest the same papal support was the visit of Pope John Paul II in 1987. A permanent observer mission of the Holy See to the United Nations keeps the Pope and his colleagues in daily contact with the world body.

For the 1965 papal visit, I was a member of the lay committee assisting in some of the arrangements for the visit of Pope Paul VI to the United Nations.

There was an inordinate interest on the part of officials at the U.S. Mission to the United Nations to find out what Pope Paul VI was going to say. There was a persistent rumor that Pope Paul VI would "attack" The U.S. policy on Vietnam. I was somewhat shocked when a member of the U.S. mission staff told me that they knew that Monsignor Alberto Giovannetti had an advance copy of the Pope's speech and asked me to somehow obtain a copy for him before the Pope gave his U.N. address.

I responded negatively, saying that Monsignor Giovannetti kept the one copy either with him or under his pillow when he was sleeping. I could not be a party, therefore, to obtaining an "advance" copy of it.

Several days after the Pope's famous address to the U.N. ("No more war ... war never again!"), I asked Monsignor Giovannetti how he safeguarded his one copy of the Pope's speech. In his vest pocket, he responded, or under his pillow. I later spoke to a friend who donated a small safe to the Monsignor.

There was no diplomatic representation of the United States to the Holy See of any kind during President Johnson's Administration. Toward the end of his administration, on December 23, 1967, President Johnson made a point of stopping off in Rome on a return trip from Vietnam to "brief" the Pope.

The visit is still remembered by Vatican authorities as ill-prepared and one that Pope Paul VI was not pleased with. The United States position on Vietnam was never fully accepted by the Holy See. The contemporary interest of the Holy See in broad world issues became evident to millions with the promulgation of Pope Paul's encyclical letter *Populorum Progressio* on Easter Sunday 1967. Here he set forth, in unequivocal and dramatic terms, the concern of the Church for the peoples of Africa, Asia, and Latin America.

This historic document begins with these words:

"The development of peoples has the Church's close attention, particularly the development of those peoples who are striving to escape from hunger, misery, endemic diseases, and ignorance; of those who are looking for wider share in the benefits of civilization and a more active improvement of their human qualities."

These sentiments of Pope Paul VI were rooted in previous papal documents — *Rerum Novarum* issued by Pope Leo XIII in 1891, *Quadragesimo Anno* issued by Pope Pius XI in 1931, and Pope John XXIII's *Pacem in Terris* in 1963.

The broad Magna Carta of Pope John Paul II's *Centesimus Annus*, issued in 1991, reformulated papal thinking on these matters for the new economic circumstances in the world. The impact of this document is discussed in Chapter X.

Concern for all peoples in the world has long been a key interest of the Holy See. It is difficult to surpass the following statement by Pope Paul VI calling attention to worldwide poverty:

"Man must indeed be enabled to survive, but he must also be given the means of living fully, as a person capable of founding a family and giving his children a satisfactory upbringing; these are the tasks that call for the disinterested help of all men of good will, surpassing all differences of nation, race, culture, and religion. Moreover, the man of today ought to become more convinced of this as each day passes; it is his own existence that is at stake, and not optional assistance and emergency aid. All human resources must be mobilized, and it is not enough to give of one's possessions; one must give of the best of oneself. The peace to which the world aspires will be built only at this price because, as has rightly been said, 'development is the new name of peace.' "

Challenges Remaining

The end of superpower confrontation, combined with the end of great geographic distance whereby all countries are next-door neighbors, along with a stronger United Nations, does not mean that really tough problems do not remain in the world community. The breakout of regional troubles in the Balkans, or in the Caucasus, and the outburst of social unrest in North Africa are a few examples of the new challenges.

The Holy See, through its worldwide network, has been especially articulate in challenging the conscience of the world on the critical problems of the tremendous gaps in living standards. In fact, John Paul II and his predecessors have been the one consistent voice in doing this. In my farewell visit with the Pope on February 13, 1993, the Pope emphasized the tragedy of the triple curse of poverty, illiteracy, and disease in Africa.

This was my last official visit with the Holy Father as the U.S. Ambassador. Margaret accompanied me, and we met with him alone in his library.

He had returned a few days before from anther trip to Africa, where his last stop was Sudan. I knew that there was some controversy about the brief visit there. I congratulated him, as I felt that his candid and forceful statements to the local government on their responsibility to guarantee human rights would have the same beneficial effect that it has had in other parts of the world.

Our entire discussion with him was on human rights or the challenges in developing countries.

Before he called in the photographers for photos, the Pope stood and shook our hands. He smiled but seemed tired and fatigued. I wanted to think that it was the stress of his recent trip to Africa that made him look that way, but I left with a haunting feeling that it might be related to his July 1992 operation.

One of the assignments given to me was to increase the concern of the Holy See for state-directed terrorism like the type practiced by Libya. Washington was not pleased with the occasional contacts that Libyan government officials would have with the Vatican, although they did not have diplomatic relations.

In my conversations with Vatican officials, I never detected any sympathy for Qaddafi and his government. But the Holy See felt that it should maintain contact with governments whose policies it disapproved of in order to have some eventual influence in changing those policies. During my tour of duty from 1989 to 1993, the influence of the Holy See on Qaddafi was very minimal. This was not the case in the neighboring countries of Morocco and Egypt, where the Holy See has had and continues to have influence with those two North African governments. Increasingly dangerous in the world community is the erratic leadership present in some volatile areas of the world. While not major powers, the dictators of these countries can obtain nuclear weapons, organize state-directed terrorist operations, causing great pain and suffering outside their boundaries, and thus present a clear and present danger to world peace.

In the industrial world there is creeping hedonism which, coupled with excessive consumerism, lowers the moral quality of life in these countries. This reduces their effectiveness on the world scene as the public image conveys a selfish interest. Modern communication assures that the poor of the world will "see, feel, and hear" the wealthy who are now their next-door neighbors.

Here the United States and the Holy See have had similar opinions about the gap in world living standards. They both recognize the moral injustice and the political dangers present in such a great difference in living standards. But they differ on approach. The United States advocates assisting the developing societies to develop their own resources with their own ideas and peoples. The Holy See, on the other hand, places a greater emphasis on the redistribution of the world's resources. One of the instructions given to me by Secretary James Baker in 1989 was to influence the Holy See to emphasize programs like adopting free-market policies in the developing countries and working for a more favorable environment for the attraction of investment, business, and trade. I was told to urge the Holy See to give less emphasis to its position on the redistribution of resources and the rich nations having an obligation to assist the poor ones.

This was a matter where I had to use my own judgment, and frankly I never did urge that. I was never pressured by the White House nor Mr. Baker's office to implement that instruction, but the Department of State personnel reminded me about this several times. In all honesty, I felt this was the correct ethical position for the Pope to take, and never in any of my meetings with Vatican officials did I suggest a change in that position.

A New Opportunity

A new chance is at hand for a world community giving greater emphasis to basic moral values. The United States and the Holy See can, in their own way, set forth universal ethical and moral standards. While the end of the superpower confrontation did not end all of the world's problems, it did open up new opportunities for global cooperation that previously did not exist.

The United Nations, no longer impotent because of the Cold War confrontation, can offer a new universal leadership in ethical values. This significant change in the potential of the U.N. made the 1991 search for a new secretary general so important. The search for the secretary general who assumed this position in January 1992 resulted in the selection of a Third World leader with roots in the historic Christian, Muslim, and Jewish traditions.

Several weeks before the appointment of Dr. Boutros Boutros-Ghali of Egypt in December 1991, I attended a Vatican-connected conference on the Island of Malta. Doctor Boutros-Ghali was presented by the conference organizers (the Saint Egidio community) before the large number of leaders of nations who were there. The discreet "Roman hand" played a role in surfacing a man uniquely qualified for the U.N. position at this time in history. I was informed by Holy See officials that Dr. Boutros-Ghali was highly regarded by them. The Sovereign Military Order of Malta, a powerful Catholic religious order, also conveyed the same sentiments to me. I so informed the United States government. Papal support for the secretary general continued after he assumed his position. One of the longest meetings of Pope John Paul II occurred in April 1993 when he met with Dr. Boutros-Ghali. They reviewed a long list of international problems. Several weeks later Dr. Boutros-Ghali was the first award recipient of the Path to Peace Foundation, a Vatican-connected philanthropic organization. I read the citation, which praised his contributions to world peace. Archbishop Renato Martino, Observer of the Holy See to the United Nations, conferred the award.

As mature and responsible members of the world community, the Holy See, the United States, and the United Nations may sometimes have different opinions on how to solve world problems, but they are all motivated by their commitment to serve the international common good. These three world-related bodies will play major roles in advancing the causes of human rights, religious freedom, and political pluralism in the world. They also will be among the first to offer assistance in a humanitarian crisis. All these recent developments have enhanced the importance to the interests of the United States of the U.S. Embassy to the Holy See.

It was against this background that on April 14, 1993, I flew to Boston to meet Mayor Raymond Flynn, whom President Clinton had designated as my successor. Mayor Flynn became the fourth Ambassador of the United States to the Holy See.

Religious Affiliation and the U.S. Ambassador

My successor, the fourth Ambassador, has a full plate of challenges that the United States and the Holy See, together and in concert with the United Nations and other countries, can cooperate in resolving. In most cases there will be a convergence of positions and in approach on how to resolve problems concerning the violations of human rights and religious freedom; there will be agreement in most cases and cooperation in world problems concerned with refugee matters and development concerns in the Third World.

While I was en route from Rome to Washington in March 1993, I was preparing a recommendation that I had planned to make to President Clinton when I arrived in Washington. My plan was to recommend that he not appoint a Catholic layperson to succeed me as the Ambassador to the Holy See. The first three Ambassadors, William Wilson, Frank Shakespeare, and I, were all known as active Catholic laypersons. I frequently heard the comment that being Catholic was an informal requirement for this position. This of course is not so, as a religious requirement for any government position is against the United States Constitution. Furthermore, the Holy See has no such requirement. Several of my very senior European colleagues in the diplomatic corps, who are highly regarded by the Holy See, were members of Protestant denominations. The Egyptian ambassador, a man of real influence at the Vatican, was not Christian.

I felt that it would be harmful to create the perception that the Vatican Embassy of the United States was a Catholic domain. It is too important a position for that perception to prevail. I never had the opportunity to do this, because on March 18 (1993) I read in the *International Herald Tribune* that President Clinton had designated Boston Mayor Raymond Flynn for the position. I knew that it would be inappropriate for me to make any such recommendation after the President had announced his decision to the American people. But I believe that serious consideration should be given by the President, whoever he may be, that the fifth Ambassador of the United States to the Holy See is a prominent American who will have the trust and respect of the Holy See but who is not Catholic. Two very prominent

Americans served as Special Envoys of the United States to the Holy See — Myron Taylor and Henry Cabot Lodge. There still remains a deep appreciation for them because they were men who had the trust of the Vatican. They were respected. They were excellent diplomats. They were well-connected with the then President of the United States. And neither envoy was a Catholic.

CHAPTER III

The U.S. and the Holy See — Unsteady Contacts: 1776-1984

THE OPPORTUNITIES for the United States and the Holy See to cooperate in the promotion of human rights, religious freedom, and political pluralism are benefiting from the full diplomatic relations now existing between the two powers.

This cordial and cooperative framework did not always exist. In fact, it took 208 years for the United States to enter into full diplomatic relations with the oldest international personality in the community of nations.

In the period from 1984 to now, the list of countries having diplomatic relations with the Holy See increased to more than 145, from 120 in January 1984, when the United States formalized the diplomatic relationship.

On October 20, 1951, President Truman formally nominated General Mark Clark as the Ambassador to the Holy See. This nomination caused a storm of protest. It came not only from those who had real objections because of the church-state nature of the Holy See, but also from those with a clear prejudice against Catholics. The remarkable political fact — almost a phenomenon — is that the high level of anti-Catholicism that torpedoed the Clark nomination in 1951 had significantly subsided thirty-three years later in 1984 when President Reagan initiated the process of establishing formal diplomatic relations with the Holy See. There was still opposition in 1984, but at an insignificant level. Chapter IV will examine that period. This chapter will review the pre-1984 period.

In the first year of the United States, the new republic had contacts with the Papal States. During that period, papal authority existed, per se, over the territory of central Italy. It was a fact. However, the recognition of this fact by the United States did not include any perception of the Holy See and the unique international personality of the Pope that transcended his role as the sovereign head of a state and the head of a church. The consular relations established by the United States in

March 1797 with the Papal States, whose capital was in Rome, were reciprocated at the same consular level in 1826 when the Papal States established a consulate in New York City. President James Polk proposed in 1848 that the United States extend formal *de jure* (legal) recognition to the Papal States and appointed a charge d'affaires (a diplomatic envoy below the ambassador level). An extensive debate then took place in the Senate on whether or not this should be done. The strong advocates wanted the U.S. representative to have the full rank of minister plenipotentiary. While there was a compromise in sending in the first instance a charge d'affaires, the appointment acknowledged formal *de jure* recognition by the U.S.A. of the Papal States as a member of the community of nations.

Mr. Jacob I. Martin presented his credentials to Pope Pius IX in Rome on August 19, 1848. Seven days later, on August 26, he died of malaria. Mr. Martin was in a certain sense the first representative of the United States government accredited to the Pope. That accreditation, however, was along the traditional line of a diplomatic representative from one state to another state. At that time the recognition did not include the fact that the Pope regarded himself as the head of the Catholic Church and of the Holy See. The letter of credentials of Mr. Martin referred to the Pope as Chief of State. There was no reference to him as head of the Catholic community. But nonetheless, he was the first representative of the Government of the United States accredited to the Pope. When I arrived, I asked to visit the grave, and after some exploration we discovered the tombstone in the Protestant cemetery. It has now been arranged that on the anniversary of his death a representative of the U.S. Embassy to the Holy See places a wreath on the grave. Some ask why Mr. Martin was buried in Rome. Our research indicated that at that time the United States government only allowed one hundred dollars for all expenses connected with a funeral and the transatlantic shipment of the body to the United States. Evidently the family of Mr. Martin could not afford the extra cost, and they indicated that he should be buried in Rome.

Mr. Martin was followed in a period of nineteen years by five other diplomats. They were: Lewis Cass, Jr., 1849-1858; John P. Stockton, 1858-1861; Alexander W. Randell, 1861-1862; Richard M. Blatchford, 1862-1863; and Rufus King, 1863-1867.

Rufus King was the last minister resident to the Papal States. He left his post in August 1867. Beginning in that year, it would not have been possible to fund such a diplomatic post, as Congress in that year prohibited the financing of any diplomatic post to the Papal States. Furthermore, with the incorporation of the Papal States into Italy (following Garibaldi's unification of Italy and virtual imprisonment of Pius IX), the United States would not have had a basis for its recognition, since control of territory was an intrinsic part of its original recognition of the Papal States. The international personality role of the Holy See and the unique role of the Pope himself were not part at that time of the act of U.S. recognition.

Mr. King's departure from Rome in 1867 initiated a long interregnum of seventy-two years when the United States had no diplomatic representative to the Pope. There was little or no indication that this absence of diplomatic contact would end until the Franklin Roosevelt administration launched the concept of a "personal representative of the President." It is interesting to note that the long absence of diplomatic representation coincided with the period of strong anti-Catholicism in the United States. It was a time when increasing number of immigrants from predominantly Catholic countries were arriving, and there was a strong negative reaction against the Irish, the French, the Italians, the Spanish, and the Germans — all those from predominantly Catholic countries. The literature at the time was full of highly intemperate and in many cases vicious characterizations of the leadership of the Catholic Church. It is hard to imagine that there could have been any kind of approval by the U.S. Congress for a diplomatic representative to the Pope under the circumstances of the late nineteenth and early twentieth centuries in the United States.

Personal Representative to the Pope

President Roosevelt announced on December 24, 1939, that he intended to send a personal representative to the Pope. The same announcement also included the news that he wanted closer contacts with the leaders of the major faiths. Thus, on Christmas Eve 1939, he informed the President of the Federal Council of Churches of Christ and the President of the Jewish Theological Seminary of America that he would be maintaining contact with them on ways to promote peace.

While the announcement had a ecumenical tone and seemed appropriate for a time when a world war had already started, there was a qualitative difference between sending a personal representative to the Pope, the head of Vatican City State and the Universal Catholic Church, and maintaining contact with the head of a large American Protestant organization and a Jewish seminary in New York.

Considerable contact already had existed between the Roosevelt administration and the Vatican at the time of the 1939 announcement. The matter of the U.S.-Vatican relations was discussed in 1936 during the visit of Eugenio Cardinal Pacelli, Vatican Secretary of State at that time (and later Pope Pius XII). Cardinal Spellman, Archbishop of New York, was the leader on the American Catholic side for promoting U.S.-Vatican diplomatic relations.

Later, when Cardinal Pacelli became Pope in March 1939, President Roosevelt sent Joseph Kennedy, then the U.S. Ambassador to England, as a special representative of the United States to the papal coronation. While this was a nominal courtesy for a chief of state, there was opposition to this move, indicating that there would be opposition to any form of diplomatic representation. It is interesting to note that Cardinal Spellman never proposed diplomatic relations with the Holy See, but with Vatican City State. This proposal was easier to sell, as recognition of Vatican City State did not include directly the role of the Pope as Vicar of Christ and head of the Roman Catholic Church. Vatican City State met the traditional criteria. It had land, a government, and armed forces (the Swiss Guards).

Shortly after his announcement on Christmas Eve 1939, President Roosevelt named Myron Taylor, an Episcopalian and retired chairman of the United States Steel Corporation, to this position. A wealthy man who could serve without compensation, Myron Taylor had a villa in Florence and knew the Pope. He was also a personal friend of the President.

The Vatican regarded Mr. Taylor as an ambassador because he represented the President of the United States. The American Constitutional requirement that the Senate must consent to all such appointments if he is as to serve as ambassador extraordinary and plenipotentiary of the United States did not seem a concern to the Vatican in 1939. Given the situation in the world in 1939 and the power of the United States, there was clear happiness in the Vatican that there would be a direct diplomatic connection with the United States government.

There was considerable opposition in the United States to Roosevelt's appointment. But since the appointment did not require Senate approval, there was no way to focus a national campaign against it. Some of the opposition was rooted in sincere concern about the constitutional implication of the appointment. Many did not understand the role of the Pope as a world leader, or as a sovereign head of the Holy See, which included Vatican City State.

Few took the pains to point out that the recognition of other leaders who also had important roles as heads of churches or religious leaders, such as (at that time) the emperor of Japan, the king of Saudi Arabia, the emperor of Ethiopia, and the English monarch, did not prevent their recognition as leaders of sovereign states.

And, of course, there was the clear case of unabashed anti-Catholicism. Catholics were still a small minority in the United States. Furthermore, many of them were either the first or second generation of immigrants. In addition to being a minority, Catholics were also insignificant in terms of wealth. In 1939 Catholics were not members of the American political-power establishment.

President Roosevelt was able to handle the opposition of all groups, because the growing war clouds in Europe diverted the attention of the public to more pressing events — and, again, the appointment did not require the consent of the Senate. Consequently there was no public forum to debate the merits of President Roosevelt's action.

Once he arrived in Rome, Myron Taylor was always treated as an Ambassador representing the Government of the United States. Taylor's ten years as his country's diplomatic envoy covered the World War II years. He had easy access to the Pope and top Vatican officials. His office was a source of invaluable information to the United States. He was able to influence the Holy See to immediately recognize in 1945 the danger of Soviet communist expansion. This led to a long period of cooperation between the United States and the Holy See on fighting the expansion of communism in Europe and in other parts of the world.

For some reason, the records of Myron Taylor's activities in Rome during World War II have not all been made available for public inspection either in U.S. archives or in the archives of the Vatican. One very persistent report that I was not able to verify was that the Japanese government in early 1945 was in contact with the Vatican to see if Pope Pius XII could serve as an intermediary to arrange a cessation of hostilities between Japan and the Allies.

Little interest, the reports state, was indicated by Mr. Taylor in the

Japanese efforts for a negotiated cessation of hostilities. President Roosevelt was determined to obtain unconditional and total surrender of both the Japanese and the Germans. Roosevelt's unconditional-surrender doctrine was not consistent with the Vatican's just-war beliefs.

President Truman's Nomination of General Clark

Following Myron Taylor's retirement in 1949, President Harry Truman waited until 1951 to name a successor. He made the decision to do what President Roosevelt did not do. President Truman nominated General Mark Clark as the first Ambassador to the Vatican. Here again, the emphasis in President Truman's nomination was on the independence of Vatican City State. It was not related to the very specific role of the Pope as head of the Holy See and the worldwide Catholic community.

This action came after eighty-three years of no official government-to-government diplomatic representation of the U.S. government with the Holy See. The last diplomatic representative of the Government of the United States to the Papal States had left Rome in 1870. Myron Taylor was the personal representative of the President to the Pope and thus had no formal government position. He could speak for the President but could not speak for or commit the United States government.

Some thought that President Truman's decision came after careful analysis of the mood of the country. Others commented that he was interested in influencing the Catholic vote in the 1952 elections.

In any case, opposition to the nomination mounted quickly, and it was more intense than President Truman had expected. While there was some question about the qualification of General Clark for the post, others were strongly opposed to the "recognition" by the U.S. government of a "church." While it is true that the concept of the sovereignty of the Holy See rather than the independence of Vatican City State was not clearly explained, a major obstacle to the confirmation was bitter anti-Catholicism.

The National Council of Churches declared the nomination to be a "threat to basic American principles" and formally asked President Truman to cancel the nomination. The issue aroused such emotion that the ecumenically based National Council of Christians and Jews expressed public concern that the proposed appointment was energizing bitter interdenominational feelings. The failure of the Clark nomination was caused by three factors. The lack of groundwork by President Truman's staff and the desire of General Clark to maintain his military rank were two of the factors.

But the high pitch of religious opposition — some based on honest concern about the separation of church and state, and the rest mainly on religious prejudice — was a major factor in the defeat. President Truman and the staff misjudged the character of the opposition. Strong mainstream Protestant groups still had prejudices against Catholicism. The opposition was from the center of American political life, not just from religious extremes. Proposals opposed by the American political center normally are not adopted.

I was a graduate student majoring in government at that time at the Catholic University of America in Washington, D.C. Never ever thinking that I would one day be the Ambassador of the United States to the Holy See, I attended several of the rallies against the appointment in 1952. I was curious about what the reasons were. It was my first direct contact with the public manifestation of religious bias against my own faith. The hatred and fear expressed toward Catholics was similar to the "Pope-baiting" that had greeted Al Smith's candidacy for President in the 1920s. As a young person growing up in eastern Connecticut, I had heard "wisecracks" and jokes from individuals against Catholics, but this was the first time I saw bigotry articulated to a large audience. While there were and still are some who have rational objections to diplomatic relations based on their interpretation of the U.S. Constitution, there was little rationality in the 1952 Washington rallies against President Truman's appointment.

Return to Personal Representative

In 1952, President Truman had decided not to submit the Clark nomination to the formal confirmation process. Another eighteen years would expire before a U.S. President would attempt to name any kind of a senior diplomat to the Holy See. There was no diplomatic representative in the administrations of Presidents Eisenhower, Kennedy, and Johnson.

President Nixon broke the long interregnum in 1969 and appointed Henry Cabot Lodge as his personal representative to the Pope. Mr. Lodge, a former U.S. Senator, had the courtesy title of "Ambassador," as he had served as U.S. Ambassador to the United Nations, Vietnam, and Germany. Ambassador Lodge assumed his part-time responsibilities on June 5, 1970, and served until July 6, 1977. Vietnam, the spread of independence in Africa, and Cuba were among the major topics that Ambassador Lodge took up with Vatican officials.

Shortly after his inaugural, President Carter filled the appointment quickly, and David Walters served as the personal representative of the President from July 6, 1977, until August 18, 1978. This brief period of service was followed by President Carter's appointment of a well-known political figure, Robert F. Wagner, former mayor of the City of New York, on November 28, 1978. He served as a personal representative of the President until 1981 and devoted many efforts to the problems of United States Embassy hostages in Iran.

Last Personal Representative

President Ronald Reagan continued the practice of naming a personal representative to the Pope. Within a few weeks of his election in November 1980, he announced that he would name William A. Wilson of California to that position.

A longtime friend and associate of Ronald Reagan, Ambassador Wilson assumed his duties in early 1981. It soon became apparent that he would devote considerable time and attention to a position that many in the Department of State regarded as "part-time."

Although it is noteworthy now, in light of President Reagan's subsequent decision to upgrade the diplomatic post to Ambassador plenipotentiary and extraordinary of the U.S. government, it was not immediately noticed that the State Department was giving the Personal Representative more support than his predecessors received. Furthermore, President Reagan's support for a significant diplomatic presence at the Holy See was soon evident. President Reagan's very important meeting with Pope John Paul II on June 7, 1982 established the groundwork for U.S.-Vatican cooperation in ending communist control, first in Poland and then in the rest of Eastern Europe.

Within a year of the President's inaugural, it became known that the national security advisor, Mr. William Clark, was making a study of the matter of diplomatic relations with the Holy See. The study and consultations took around three years. The Senate was consulted, and the leaders of the various religious communities were asked for their opinions. Given the recent history of the contemporary controversies that surrounded President Roosevelt's nomination of a personal envoy in 1939, and

President Truman's failed attempt to nominate an Ambassador of the United States for senate approval, the Reagan administration moved carefully on this project. As we will see in the next chapter, the professional approach by the President and his staff and the significant change in the sociopolitical and religious climate made it possible for the United States in 1984 to establish formal diplomatic ties with the Holy See. Previous relationships of the Special Envoy to the Pope and the diplomatic representative to the Papal States in the nineteenth century avoided recognizing the Holy See in a clear, precise way. All this changed on January 10, 1984 when President Reagan established diplomatic relations with the Holy See.

CHAPTER IV

The U.S. and the Holy See — A Firm Commitment in 1984

O N JANUARY 10, 1984, President Ronald Reagan announced the establishment of formal diplomatic relations with the Holy See. Some would say the "reestablishment" of diplomatic relations, because, as the previous chapter indicated, the United States had had diplomatic relations with the Papal States in the nineteenth century. Beginning with President Roosevelt in 1939, the President of the United States had frequently had a personal representative to the Pope. The Pontiff's being head of Vatican City was one principal reason for this special diplomatic relationship.[1]

The 1984 announcement by President Reagan, however, gave full recognition to the unique international sovereign role of the Pope and his government, not only in Vatican City State but throughout the world where the Pope and his government exercised their spiritual and political authority. There was no equivocation in this announcement. The United States was extending full recognition for the first time to the government of the Holy Catholic and Apostolic Church.

The study conducted by the National Security Council at the request of President Reagan indicated strong bipartisan and ecumenical support for the establishment of diplomatic relations and clearly established its legitimacy, in terms of the United States Constitution and international law. There was however opposition to the move within the Department of State. Then Secretary of State George Schultz had serious reservations about the proposal.

---

[1] An unusual situation existed during World War II when President Roosevelt, under the wartime powers act, requested the Holy See to list a diplomat of the U.S. Embassy to Italy as one of the diplomats accredited to the Holy See. This action by the Vatican protected him from being imprisoned by the government of Italy, which was then in a state of war with the United States. Subsequent to this action, however, neither the U.S. nor the Holy See regarded it as the establishment of diplomatic relations. It was a favor granted to the United States by the Holy See during a time of war.

But the White House support was led by President Reagan and the Security Council; Judge William Clark, national security advisor, General Alexander Haig, who had preceded Schultz as Secretary of State, and William Casey, director of the Central Intelligence Agency, were strong supporters of the proposed diplomatic recognition. Ambassador William Wilson was in many ways the quarterback of the campaign. His close friendship with Ronald Reagan gave him easy access to the President. When the recognition project was held up by the Department of State in the fall of 1983 Mr. Wilson fought hard to get it moving. When finally he couldn't do that, he personally appealed to President Reagan. Following Ambassador Wilson's personal appeal in December 1983, President Reagan made his decision to proceed with the appointment.

In the announcement of January 10, 1984, President Reagan simultaneously nominated William A. Wilson, who had been serving as his personal envoy, as the first U.S. Ambassador extraordinary and plenipotentiary to the Holy See. He was to be the Ambassador of the United States with full ambassadorial powers, and he was to be accredited to the Holy See.

The fairly rapid confirmation of Ambassador Wilson surprised many observers. His confirmation was not so much an examination of his credentials as a review of fundamental constitutional issues of church and state. It was also a test of ecumenical relationships. The 1951 nomination of General Mark Clark by President Truman, only thirty-three years before, had energized deep anti-Catholic feelings. It had been feared that this could occur again.

In fact, the stinging defeat of the 1951 attempt to name an Ambassador to the Holy See had been followed nine years later in 1960 by the first Roman Catholic president, John F. Kennedy, who bluntly stated his opposition to such a move.

"I believe that the separation of church and state is fundamental to our American concept and heritage and should remain so. I am flatly opposed to the appointment of an Ambassador to the Vatican. Whatever advantages it might have in Rome, and I am not convinced of these, they would be more than offset by the divisive effects at home."[2]

---

[2] Committee On Foreign Relations, United States Senate, February 1, 1984, p. 20.

President Kennedy continued his total opposition to any diplomatic contact with the Holy See by not continuing even the tradition of naming a special envoy. Vatican officials told me how shocked their predecessors were by this action of the Kennedy Administration.

At no time, they told me, did any member of the Kennedy Administration give a rationale for the coldness that existed toward the Holy See.

The Reagan staff, aware of these past failures and circumstances, made extensive studies of the subject. This review included the power of the President. Section 2, Article 2 of the Constitution defines the President's authority to nominate diplomatic officials and the responsibility of the Senate to give its consent. There never was any question in the mind of President Reagan's counsel that the President had the power to recognize the Holy See as an international personality and thus to nominate an Ambassador of the United States to represent the government and to receive an Ambassador from the Holy See.

A big question was rooted in domestic politics. The opposition to Truman's nomination of General Clark was in many ways vicious. The only Catholic President, John F. Kennedy, would not subsequently even review that proposal. In fact, he blocked an attempt to reopen the matter.

The legal situation had not changed in the 1980s, but the domestic political climate had. Dr. Billy Graham stated publicly that he saw a significant difference in the national Protestant attitude. There was still opposition, but not as vehement as it had been thirty years previously.

First Steps by Reagan

Once he was convinced that the nomination of an Ambassador to the Holy See was constitutional and in the national interest of the country, President Reagan approved a move to void the 1868 law which prohibited the expenditure of public funds for an Embassy to the Vatican. This action was successful. The relative ease with which this action took place reassured the Reagan White House about proceeding with their project.

The administration, now ready to initiate the process, approached the Holy See. President Reagan took advantage of being in the same hotel with Cardinal Casaroli, then Secretary of State for the Holy See, at the hundredth anniversary convention of the Knights of Columbus in September 1982 in Hartford, Connecticut, and informed Cardinal Casaroli of the U.S. intentions. Mindful of the embarrassment caused by

Truman's ill-fated undertaking in 1951 and the strong opposition of Kennedy in 1960, Cardinal Casaroli received the information politely but without much comment. He may have been fearful that anti-Catholicism was still a strong factor in American politics. Cardinal Casaroli and his advisors refrained from saying anything publicly about the possibility of establishing diplomatic relations. They were frankly dubious, in view of the recent past, that it could be done.

January 10, 1984

Once the announcement was made on January 10, 1984, that the United States would establish diplomatic relations with the Holy See, and that the President would nominate William A. Wilson to serve as the first Ambassador, the opposition became public. The announcement implied the acceptance of the international-law principle that the Holy See is a bona fide international personality. Thus the announcement by President Reagan acknowledged the papacy as a religious organ with international rights and duties. This was not a qualified recognition of Vatican City State. In previous times it would have caused a firestorm of protest. But it immediately became evident, both in tone and substance, that there had been a major change in domestic U.S. political opinion. There was some opposition, however.

The opposition in the 1984 hearings fell into three groups:

1. Those who sincerely doubted the constitutionality of the action.
2. Those who exhibited clear anti-Catholic prejudice.
3. Catholics opposed to the nomination for fear that the U.S. government would use official pressure to influence religious and/or state and/or church decisions of the Vatican.

Legal Challenges

As soon as the Senate approved (by a landslide vote) the establishment of full diplomatic relations with the Holy See and the nomination of William A. Wilson as the U.S. Ambassador, several legal suits were initiated. Their purpose was to have the courts declare the action to be null and void. The suits were not taken seriously by the courts, and they were all dismissed. Petitioners seeking to void the decisions of the President and the Congress included two Roman Catholic groups. When Frank Shakespeare was nominated in 1986 to succeed

Ambassador Wilson, a suit to void his nomination was also initiated, but it too was dismissed. He took the oath of office on January 8, 1987.

Following my nomination by President Bush on June 9, 1989, I prepared for my confirmation hearings by studying all of the constitutional issues. There was no discussion of this aspect before the committee. Senator Joseph Biden, who presided at my committee hearing, recognized two groups that objected to the appointment of an Ambassador to the Holy See. They were invited to submit their reports. The committee subsequently voted unanimously in favor of my nomination.

From the time President Bush discussed this appointment with me, I felt strongly that the Ambassador to the Holy See should have very strong bipartisan and ecumenical support. My two democratic Senators, Christopher J. Dodd and Joseph Lieberman of Connecticut, one a Catholic layman and the other a Jewish layman, provided an impetus to this goal by their immediate and strong endorsement of my nomination. There was no opposition to my nomination in the full Senate.

The ease with which my 1989 nomination passed the Senate was reflective of the national public opinion. I received supporting letters from leaders of the Protestant, Jewish, and Orthodox Churches and of course from my own. The support from the Catholic community was overwhelming. There was no opposition of any significance, and there was no attempt to initiate judicial action against the appointment.

The United States, after a long wait and bitter arguments, joined most of the nations of the world in 1984 and exchanged ambassadors with the Holy See. The acceptance of this reality was then again confirmed in the Senate hearings for Frank Shakespeare in 1986 and for me in 1989.

This new relationship came at a time when the world witnessed the ending of the Soviet superpower status in the world and the transformation of repressive authoritarian regimes in Eastern Europe, Latin American, and Africa.

These governments pledged to guarantee human rights, religious freedom, and political pluralism. New conflicts developed as old ones were resolved, but now the United States and the Holy See were able to work together directly in attempting to resolve them.

My tour of duty, starting in mid-1989, coincided with the dramatic changes occurring in Central and Eastern Europe and in the Soviet Union. Both the Holy See and the United States played significant roles in this transformation, and it was clearly facilitated by the existence of full diplomatic relations.

When I completed my mission in March 1993, the U.S. Embassy to the Holy See was slightly more than nine years old. It was clear that in these nine years that the U.S. Embassy had established itself as an embassy that followed the American tradition of separation of church and state. I knew when I arrived at the post in 1989 that there were still those who were suspicious that "somehow, somewhere" the United States Embassy to the Holy See would become involved in church and/or religious matters. The Holy Father, in his role as a religious leader, would of course speak on religious subjects. Some of them would be classified as controversial: e.g., abortion, sexual ethics, eugenics, or gay rights. Every time this happened I would receive an inquiry from a newspaper or from the TV-radio media. There was never any question of my responding, because these were Church matters and as such were not appropriate ones for the United States Ambassador to comment on. Also, in the course of each of my years, there would be actions on the Church side of the Holy See concerning the appointments of bishops, archbishops, and cardinals. Again there would be inquiries about whether they were "too conservative or too liberal." Here again, I maintained the very strict rule that there be absolutely no comment on internal Church matters at the U.S. Embassy.

I remember one particular incident in the weeks approaching May 1992. The beatification of Josémaría Escrivá de Balaguer, the founder of Opus Dei, sparked varying opinions of approval and disapproval. I normally responded by saying, "This is a Church matter, and it would not be appropriate for the U.S. Ambassador to discuss the merits of it." On a personal basis, I knew the work of Opus Dei and was pleased with the decision of the Church to designate Monsignor Escrivá as "Blessed," but I only said this privately to a few personal friends.

This church-state separation continued the tradition established by Benjamin Franklin in the very early days of the Republic. He was approached in Paris by a papal envoy who wished to tell him about the desire of the Pope to appoint a bishop for the Catholics in the new United States. Ambassador Franklin responded that this was not necessary and that it was not an appropriate subject for discussion by a U.S. government official.

Father John Carroll subsequently was appointed Bishop of Baltimore in 1789 by Pope Pius VI. Many decades later, President Franklin

Roosevelt thought he could influence Pope Pius XII on an appointment. In a message to the Pope, he urged that Auxiliary Bishop Bernard Shiel of Chicago be named the first Archbishop of Washington. Pope Pius XII never responded, and Bishop Shiel remained an auxiliary bishop.

There have been very few departures by the U.S. government from the Benjamin Franklin tradition of staying strictly out of Catholic Church business. In fact the attempt by President Roosevelt is the only known attempt by the U.S government to influence an episcopal appointment.

During my four years in Rome, I became very involved in commenting on the diplomatic activities of the Holy See in the fields of human rights, religious freedom, political pluralism, and the whole area of humanitarian affairs. Furthermore, the Holy See was frequently active in issuing statements on problems of refugees and world health matters. These were all appropriate matters for the United States Embassy to report on and to be active in. The tradition now has been firmly established that the Embassy of the Government of the United States is very sensitive to the Constitution and to the American traditions of church-state separation, and we maintain appropriate diplomatic relations with the government of the Holy See.

CHAPTER V

Eastern Europe: From Communist Domination to Independence

O N DECEMBER 14, 1991, I attended the closing session of the European synod. Presided over by the Pope, representatives of the Church from all parts of Europe met together for two weeks in Vatican City. While synods were normally primarily church functions which I would not attend, I made an exception for this one because of overriding political implications. Delegates were there from the Catholic churches in Lithuania, Russia, Ukraine, Romania, Czechoslovakia, Hungary, Bulgaria, and other areas meeting side by side with church leaders from Western Europe.

Western European prelates in well-fitting clerical clothes mixed with their brother bishops from Eastern Europe, who were in many cases wearing cassocks just recently purchased. Only several years previously, some of the same Eastern European church leaders had been imprisoned or confined to limited geographic areas. For the first time some of the Eastern European church leaders were learning about post-World War II developments, Vatican Council II changes, and the progress made in pluralism, ecumenism, and interreligious dialogue.

The leading experts of the time said that the communist domination of Eastern Europe was a fact of life and would last forever, and that there was no hope that the Christian communities could ever practice Christianity at their previous level. It is difficult to find anyone who is on record in the 1970s, or in fact the early 1980s, as having confidence that a European community comprising the Eastern and Western parts would evolve by this century. Those who heard the words of Pope John Paul II in 1979, calling for a united Europe, thought that they were the ideas of a well-meaning religious leader but had no possibility of coming to fruition.

The Pope's prophetic remarks were made in 1979, when the world was deeply enmeshed in the Cold War. U.S. and Western policy focus was on military preparedness against the Soviet Union. There was little hope that the Eastern European countries would ever regain their freedom. Pope John Paul II's commitment to bring freedom to Eastern

Europe was reinforced by President Reagan's determination to do the same. This convergence of determination, occurring in the beginning of the 1980s, brought results by the end of that decade. In 1979-1980, the expert advisers to Pope John Paul II and President Reagan warned them against encouraging the peoples behind the "Iron Curtain" to seek freedom.

But the Pope and President Reagan thought otherwise, and their convergence on this matter was the basis of an understanding that facilitated the march to freedom in the captive nations.

Beginning in December 1990, many of my contacts at the Vatican were with Archbishop Jean-Louis Tauran. This French prelate was elevated to high rank in his late forties. He previously had served in Lebanon and was a specialist in Arab culture. Some diplomats warned me that he was cool to American policies. I never found this to be true. Upon leaving the Vatican in 1993, I regarded him as an extraordinarily competent senior official of the Holy See.

A cultured man who is able to go immediately to the issue under discussion, he relaxes at the piano, as he is an accomplished pianist.

Poland

The Iron Curtain was brutal in its separation of Europe into two unfriendly camps. But as already noted, the Pope in the late 1970s predicted that a democratic community would emerge and unite all of Europe.

During his first trip to Poland in June 1979, a decade before the fall of the Berlin Wall, Pope John Paul II spoke of a united Christian Europe. In his speech to the Polish Bishops Conference, he said: "Europe — which during its history was many times divided — can now cease to seek its fundamental unity and must address itself to Christianity. Despite the different traditions that exist between its Eastern and Western parts, there is in those traditions Christianity. . . ."

The Pope's clear call for a European community that would be free of the then hard divisions caused by the Soviet communist domination of Eastern Europe was mostly unnoticed.

This papal call for a European community in 1979 was preceded by a five-year period of regular contacts between Poland and the Holy See. But starting with the 1979 visit, it was obvious that the Pope was committed to a far more active role in obtaining freedom for Poland. The

Pope was the quarterback of the game to restore freedom to his homeland.

He made three trips to Poland, before the opening of Eastern Europe, in 1979, 1983 and 1987. His visits gave hope to a nation oppressed by communism. He energized the changes that led to the 1989-1990 period when Poland was transformed from a communist state to a democratic one.

In 1981 the Pope received Lech Walesa as head of *Solidarnosc* during the period of the Gdansk strikes. During the momentous years of the 1980s, both the United States and the Holy See spoke out and assisted the "Solidarity-Freedom movement" in Poland.

On June 7, 1982, an historic meeting took place between President Reagan and Pope John Paul II in Vatican City. It was at this meeting that President Reagan raised the question of what the Pope thought about freeing Eastern Europe from communist domination. President Reagan came to the meeting determined that many of the experts in his own government were wrong. These experts advised him that things would not change in Eastern Europe and that in fact it was dangerous even to promote it. They pointed out the catastrophic suffering that was caused by the attempted revolts against communist domination in Poland, Hungary, and East Germany in the 1950s and the 1960s. But President Reagan nonetheless believed that things could change. One of his aides gave him a copy of the remarks made by the Pope in his 1979 visit to Poland. And President Reagan raised the question. He frankly asked the Holy Father if he thought that freedom could be restored in those parts of Eastern Europe behind the Iron Curtain.

The Pope responded with a smile. And he said freedom could be obtained in their lifetimes. This was the beginning of an extended conversation where the Pope and the President discussed their goals for restoring human rights and religious freedom not only to Poland but to Eastern Europe, and by implication to the Soviet Union. The meeting in 1982 took place approximately a year after both President Reagan and Pope John Paul II were the victims of assassination attempts. They both were shot and could easily have been killed. Both survived, and both had the feeling that it was part of their mission to restore human rights and religious freedom to Eastern Europe.

Following this historic 1982 meeting in Vatican City, there was close cooperation between the Holy See and the United States on matters of strategy. It was one of the most successful cooperative diplomatic efforts in history.

While I was preparing for my assignment in the spring of 1989, I could sense from reading the files that those initial contacts in the first several years of President Reagan's first term established the basis for a very close working relationship between Washington and the Vatican. This was done while William Wilson was still a special envoy. The combination of Alexander Haig as Secretary of State, William Clark as Assistant to the President for National Security Affairs, Bill Wilson, and the deep interest of President Reagan assured that this new era of cooperation on strategy would move ahead. On the Vatican side, Archbishop Pio Laghi, who at the time had no diplomatic status, represented the Pope in Washington and was a strong link. Within eight years freedom occurred in Poland, due in great measure to that cooperation between the Holy See and the United States.

On July 17, 1989, Poland was the first of the then communist-bloc countries to reestablish diplomatic relations with the Holy See. Several weeks later, in August, the Pope received Mr. Walesa during his campaign for the presidency. Shortly before the November 1990 elections in Poland, he remarked that Poland's presidential candidates should work together for the country's welfare. Rome was full of anticipation when I arrived there in the summer of 1989. In my meeting with the Pope on October 2, he expressed his appreciation for the assistance being given by the United States to the independence movement. He had a complete mastery of the facts. I told him that the Embassy would stay in close communication with his subordinates on all matters involving Poland.

I felt it important that I acquire some sense of what was going on in Poland, and the Department of State granted me permission to visit Poland in August 1990. I had several long discussions with Cardinal Macharski, Archbishop of Krakow, and his senior aides. Our visit to the area of Krakow — the seat of Catholic culture in Poland — revealed a great deal about the historic Catholic traditions of Poland and how they were able to withstand both the Nazi and communist periods of domination. That strong cultural base provided a firm framework for the transition from communist domination to democratic institutions in 1989-1990.

There was no question in my mind that the transformation of Poland from a communist-dominated state to a democratic society was largely brought about by the leadership of Pope John Paul II. Once this process was set in motion, the movement for change continued in Eastern Europe.

The understanding between President Reagan and Pope John Paul II later emerged into a Pope John Paul II convergence with Gorbachev that facilitated the sweeping changes of 1989-1992.

There was an obvious parallelism of interest between the United States and the Holy See in their policies toward Eastern Europe. The Holy See took the lead in Poland and then, working through its network, energized the impetus for freedom in other Eastern European countries. The information given to us was very valuable. My deputy chief of mission, my political officer, and I were forwarding reports with information about Eastern European developments to Washington on a weekly basis.

This occurred at a time when the peoples of these countries were suffering from the harshness and the loneliness of the failed communist system. The one major domestic institution that was with them in their desperate years was the Catholic Church. All throughout this period the Church advocated values of human rights and religious freedom — all values so strongly denied by the communists.

The Convent at Auschwitz

When I was preparing for my assignment in the spring of 1989, a problem was evolving over a Carmelite convent at Auschwitz. Auschwitz is that horrible place where at least 1.5 million Jews were killed during the period of the Nazi occupation. It was a manifest example of genocide. I knew something of the history. In preparing for my assignment, I noticed that there was resentment in the Jewish community that the Carmelite sisters were preparing a convent to engage in prayer in one of the original buildings of the old concentration-camp facility. In discussing the matter with State Department officials before departing in the summer of 1989 for my position in Rome, I was told that this was primarily a "church matter" and therefore not one appropriate for me to become involved in. However, within several weeks of my arrival in August 1989, I received word that the challenging problem of the convent at Auschwitz was disturbing relations between the State of Israel and Poland, that various Jewish leaders throughout the world were deeply concerned about it, and that I should quietly see what I could do to find out what role the Holy See could play in this sensitive situation.

Since I had not yet presented my credentials to the Pope, I was restricted as to what I could do in August-September 1989. I hesitated at first, but the newspaper headlines vividly indicated that the situation was getting worse. At first it was difficult for me to understand why the prayerful actions of fourteen Carmelite nuns could be viewed so badly by the Jewish community. And there was a growing negative reaction from Jewish leaders throughout the world.

I was in contact with my friends at the American Jewish Committee. Rabbi James Rudin came to Rome in September for a visit. I told Jim that I was the Ambassador of all Americans and I wanted to work in an even-handed way to find a just and fair solution to this controversy.

He briefed me on how the worldwide Jewish community viewed Auschwitz. That tragedy had resulted in a state of perpetual mourning for all Jewish people. In such circumstances no other religious groups should interfere or be involved, even though well-intentioned. There was a clash of symbols. The months went on, and there was really no definite solution. I also discussed the problem with Rabbi Leon Klenicki of the Anti-Defamation League and Rabbi Arthur Schneier of the Appeal of Conscience Foundation.

I decided that I should visit Auschwitz myself to see what the circumstances were like. I am very pleased that I did, because then I was able to comprehend the enormity of this tragedy. It was a most depressing experience; the moment we arrived, my wife and I felt that we too were in mourning. We saw with our own eyes the railroad tracks where thousands and thousands of Jews were brought in trains and then separated: those to be executed immediately and those who could work for a while before execution at another nearby concentration camp — Birkenau. Probably the most striking aspect of this grotesque human tragedy was the fact that the documentation revealed that it was all planned. There were detailed diagrams of how the train came in and what happened. There were not too many names, because if you were Jewish you were given a number — not a name. We visited the wall of death and placed some flowers there. It was a very grim day, and as we were leaving in the afternoon we actually bumped into some people that we knew. Again we felt we were in mourning. We were not able to speak to them. We left quickly and quietly. On the return trip, Margaret and I both thought we could hear the screams of Auschwitz.

When I returned to Rome, I met with Vatican officials and gave my own strong personal opinion: I felt that even though others had been killed at Auschwitz, and that included thousands and thousands of

Christians, the overwhelming majority were Jewish people, and they were killed because they were Jewish, in a clear-cut plan of genocide. We therefore should allow the Jewish people to mourn, and we should be very sensitive to what they wanted. Even though the efforts of the Carmelite sisters, inspired by a Catholic tradition, were very well-intended, it was really offensive to the Jewish community.

I felt that I had some influence in transmitting this information to Vatican officials, but I must confess that in discussing it with other visiting Americans I did not find too many who had not visited Auschwitz who could understand the sensitivity of the Jewish community. I continued to press my point informally with key Vatican leaders. I knew that probably it never would be resolved by local Polish civic and religious leaders, and therefore I was pleased when in April 1993 the Pope took the matter into his own hands and ordered the Carmelite sisters to leave the Auschwitz area.

The Baltic States

The Soviet takeover of Lithuania, Latvia, and Estonia was never recognized by the Holy See and the United States. Once the Soviets absorbed the three Baltic states in 1945, a very harsh period of oppression for Catholics started. As the success of the Holy Father's call for freedom in Poland became apparent in the late 1980s, the long-suppressed aspirations of the Baltic peoples began to emerge. And changes, at first slowly, began to occur.

Lithuania was the Baltic state with the most significant Catholic population. Despite the Soviet oppression, the Holy See always maintained contact with the clergy there. This was helped by the well-organized church underground in neighboring Poland.

In 1988, Bishop Julijonas Steponavicius, who was not allowed to carry out his duties as apostolic administrator of Vilnius, was allowed to leave the country and meet with the Pope on October 8. The movement for freedom gained momentum after that. In the June 1988 consistory, Vincentas Sladkevicius, rehabilitated under Gorbachev after thirty years in exile, was named a cardinal and head of the newly reconstituted Lithuanian Bishops Conference.

Not wanting to destabilize Gorbachev in the critical 1989-1990 period, the Holy See, like the United States, urged patience and restraint during these months of nationalist uprisings. There was never any question that both the United States and the Holy See were fully committed to independence and sovereignty for Lithuania, Latvia, and Estonia.

I kept the Holy See informed of developments so that full independence for the Baltic states should occur in such a way as not to destroy the sometimes fragile democracy movement in Moscow. Both Washington and the Holy See wanted the transition to full freedom and independence to occur with an absolute minimum of bloodshed.

The Baltic strategy was successful. The United States, the Holy See, and the then Soviet Union recognized Lithuania, Latvia, and Estonia in August-September 1991.

During the 1990 transition period, I was subject to pressure from Lithuanian-American friends. I had established the Center for Ethnic Studies at Sacred Heart University in Connecticut, which had a Lithuanian-American community, and therefore knew many of the Lithuanian Catholic leaders. They wrote to me. Some came to Rome to visit me expressing disappointment at the tardiness of both the United States government and the Holy See in not pushing faster for full recognition of Lithuania's independence in 1990. It was hard to dialogue with them on the matter. They felt very strongly and did not seem to be concerned about the fact that rushing the independence in 1990 could have resulted in the fall of Gorbachev.

There was later concern in 1993 when the Lithuanian people elected Algirdas Brazauskas as president of the republic. The country in 1992 had undergone some very difficult economic times. Mr. Brazauskas had in the previous era been an active communist leader. Again I was contacted by some of the same Lithuanian-American friends, who feared that the country was reverting to communism. In my discussion with Holy See leaders, I found them relaxed on this matter. They felt that the traditionally strong Catholic culture would protect the Lithuanian people from domination by a local communist government. They distinguished from the old days when the communist government was the result of Soviet domination. I transmitted these feelings and impressions of the Holy See to Washington and found that there was a general concurrence. Lithuania was free; so were the other two Baltic states, and there was little danger of their reverting back to a communist-dominated empire.

My wife and I visited Lithuania for a month from mid-December

1993 to mid-January 1994. The Lithuanian people are carrying scars of the past.

There was the centuries-old oppressive domination of Czarist Russia. Following independence after World War I, Poland seized the historic capital of Vilnius. The infamous Hitler-Stalin pact was signed in 1939. The major Western powers did little to prevent the Nazis and communists from dividing up Eastern Europe and the Baltic states.

Following the cruel Nazi occupation when the Jewish population of around 235,000 was almost entirely wiped out during World War II, the Soviets arrived. Lithuanians believed that the West, especially the United States, would not allow the Soviets to reimpose a long, oppressive regime on the Lithuanians, who had very unpleasant memories of the first Soviet invasion of 1940-41. For over eight years, 1945-53, Lithuanian freedom fighters fought bravely against the vastly superior Soviet military. Over 35,000 were killed and many more exiled, never to return.

By mid-1950 it had become apparent that the West would follow through on capitulation to Stalin's demands at Yalta and thus abandon Lithuania and the other Baltic states to Soviet tyranny.

My talks with Lithuanian leaders from all walks of life strongly indicated their appreciation for the role of Pope Pius XII. He opposed the betrayal of Eastern and Central Europe's peoples to the Soviet communists. During the dark forty-five-year period of Soviet occupation, the Vatican helped the Catholic community in every way possible.

The visit of Pope John Paul II September 4-8, 1993, was a remarkable event. The papal visit occurred several days after withdrawal of the last Russian army units. His visit was welcomed with great enthusiasm. He preached reconciliation and said optimistically that "Lithuania will be able to embark upon the road of rebuilding unity in peaceful cooperation with the other nations of Europe."

Recognizing the tragedy of Lithuania's past, the Pope dramatically visited the Hill of Crosses in northern Lithuania. The Pontiff knew that the more than 100,000 crosses there symbolized the past Lithuanian suffering. My wife, Margaret, and I hardly ever met a Lithuanian family that did not have an experience of the KGB "knock on the door" and the consequent shipping off to Siberia of one of their relatives.

While we were visiting Lithuania, President Clinton was in Brussels, Prague, and Moscow. Quite a few Lithuanians brought up the memory of Yalta and were fearful that they could again become victims of Russian expansionism. There is no concern about former local communists in Lithuania, but the remarks by extreme nationalists in Russia about the Baltic states remaining in their sphere of influence were troubling to many Lithuanians.

Czechoslovak Federal Republic

Shortly after my arrival in Rome in August 1989, preparations had started for the canonization of Blessed Agnes of Bohemia (a princess who renounced marriage and was named an abbess by her friend Saint Clare of Assisi). The Prague government reluctantly acknowledged that this would be happening. They indicated that a handful of Czechoslovakian peoples would attend.

The old communist Czechoslovakia had been a fortress of communist oppression. In his October 1987 address to the synod of bishops, John Paul II singled out religious oppression in communist Czechoslovakia in the strongest terms. The Pope said that the absence of many Czechoslovakian bishops was an "eloquent indication of the conditions in which the church in that region lives."

At that time, ten out of thirteen episcopal sees were vacant. Between 1968 and 1988 only one bishop had been appointed. The Czech people had manifested their desire for freedom in the spring of 1968 and the uprising had been brutally suppressed.

Two years later, in 1970, my wife, young daughters, and I were in Prague on a brief vacation. The sadness of the peoples was overwhelming. But within a few years, when the sweep of freedom would spread from Poland to its neighboring countries, the attitudes changed and hope permeated the thinking of the Czechoslovakian peoples.

I witnessed this phenomenal change in attitudes as plans progressed for the canonization of Blessed Agnes. From the early predictions of the Prague government in August that only a handful would come to Rome, the numbers increased to the thousands. Within a few days of the canonization ceremony on November 12, 1989, almost ten thousand pilgrims from Czechoslovakia arrived by bus, car, train, and plane. These pilgrims, along with some of the newly appointed bishops and members of the government, were there when Pope John Paul II presided over the ceremonies.

It was a most moving experience to hear the pilgrims sing their age-old hymns in their own language. When I left the ceremonies, I said to several of my colleagues that this day was the defining moment in the struggle of the Czechoslovakian peoples for freedom. Later my wife and I visited the Hotel Columbus not far from Saint Peter's Square. The place was overwhelmed by pilgrims. In fact, the whole area facing Saint Peter's Square was just jam-packed with pilgrims, many dressed in their local costumes, most of them carrying flags, and all with a deep, joyous smile. Somehow they sensed that this day was the day when the return to freedom in Czechoslovakia started.

Two days later, on November 14, the Holy See and the Prague government initiated discussions that resulted in the reconstitution of the entire church hierarchy. Three bishops were appointed in December 1989 and one on February 7, 1990. On February 14, 1990, Paul John Paul II appointed five new bishops, to fill all thirteen of the country's dioceses for the first time in twenty years.

The sweep of events continued, and on April 19, 1990, the Holy See reestablished diplomatic relations with Czechoslovakia. Seventy-two hours later, on April 22, the Pope's "lightning" trip there (Prague, Velehrad, and Bratislava) was his first visit to the new democracies of Eastern Europe outside of Poland. It was an astonishingly successful visit in terms of the goals of the Pope. We knew at the embassy that the Pope had extraordinary influence with President Havel. He met with him and obtained the complete commitment of the President to push for full adoption of all laws guaranteeing human rights, religious freedom, and political pluralism in Czechoslovakia.

Continuing his promotion of the European community that would embrace both the Western and Eastern parts, the Pope, in Velehrad, at the tomb of Saint Methodius (whom, along with Saint Cyril, the Pope had named as co-patron saint of Europe), announced he would convoke an all-European synod on post-communist Europe. Pope John Paul II spoke on behalf of a European community — an idea similar to Gorbachev's proposal for a common European house.

It was in 1980 that the Pope had announced that Saints Cyril and Methodius were co-patrons of Europe. From the earliest days of his pontificate, he wanted to include the Slavs of Eastern Europe in his vision of a European community.

In 1992, as there was clear indication that the federation could break up into two republics — one Czech and one Slovak — I was approached by various Czech and Slovak Americans who were concerned about this breakup. It was also apparent that some of my senior colleagues in the

Department of State thought that the proposed breakup was ill-advised and could have disastrous economic effects, particularly on the Slovak peoples. However, I reported to the Department of State that the Holy See did not wish to take a position either for or against the breakup of the federation. Their one concern was that whatever happened should be in accordance with the Czechoslovakian constitution and should happen peacefully.

I also reported to the department that my meetings with Slovak leaders in Rome, arranged by Dr. Karol Kremery, had convinced me that they were strongly determined to seek independence. The Slovak leaders felt that historically they were treated as poor country cousins. I so advised Washington. The Slovak leaders also felt that they were disadvantaged going back to the earliest days of the republic following World War I. The breakup of the federation occurred on January 1, 1993, and it occurred peacefully. We now have the Czech Republic and the Slovak Republic, and both owe a great deal to Pope John Paul II for the role he played in 1989 and 1990 in successfully directing a strategy that brought independence to their peoples.

I was guided in my advice to the Department of State by my consultations with Archbishop Ján C. Korec, the Bishop of Nitra. Recently created a cardinal, he had spent a long time in communist prisons. He was known by the Holy Father and greatly respected by him. He was a leader in the church underground during the long period of communist oppression.

After he was freed from prison, where he had been secretly consecrated a bishop, he soon received the honor of a red hat from the Pope. I had met Cardinal Korec in Bratislava and Nitra in 1990, and he had visited me several times on his trips to Rome. I could see that even in this restrained and cautious man there was a deep feeling that the Slovak peoples, after centuries of domination by others, had a right to be independent and to have their own country.

Later in 1991 when Cardinal Korec visited the United States, he was given a hero's welcome by the Slovak-American communities in Ohio, Pennsylvania, and Connecticut. These Slovak-Americans clearly manifested their opinion on federation or independence. All their songs, comments, and greetings were for the Slovak Republic. Cardinal Korec was always referred to as the Slovak Cardinal. And this was over a year before the Slovak Republic came into existence.

Hungary

When then Cardinal Karol Wojtyla became Pope in October 1978, there was already a slight improvement for Catholics in Hungary. The Hungarian church had suffered persecution and surveillance. The Hungarian Primate, Cardinal Jozsef Mindszenty, was imprisoned in 1948 and, during the revolution in 1956, had escaped to the American Embassy.

But by September 1964, the Holy See and Hungary signed a protocol. This was the first agreement between the Vatican and a then Warsaw Pact country. The Holy See immediately appointed six bishops and another four in 1969.

When I visited Hungary in 1970, I observed more of a free spirit there than among the peoples in the neighboring communist states. The Hungarian people would very quietly and carefully speak with pride about their attempt to throw off the communist yoke in 1956. The atmosphere in Hungary consequently was ripe for the freedom movement in Eastern Europe launched by Pope John Paul II.

Inspired by the dramatic developments in Poland, the Holy See on September 15, 1989, on the twenty-fifth anniversary of the protocol, praised Hungary's efforts toward better church-state relations, "increasing the margin of freedom for the Church," the opening of Hungary's borders to East German refugees. Talks within weeks started on the resumption of diplomatic relations.

On February 9, 1990, full diplomatic relations were announced and on May 4 the Vatican sent a delegation to the ceremonies marking the return of the remains of Cardinal Jozsef Mindszenty to the Cathedral in Esztergom. Americans at the ceremony included Frank Shakespeare, a former U.S. ambassador to the Holy See (1987-1989), who on behalf of President Nixon had played a role in obtaining safe passage for the Hungarian cardinal so he could leave the American Embassy in October 1971.

The May ceremonies were followed in July by an agreement whereby religious education would be reintroduced as an option in primary and secondary schools. Pope John Paul II's visit to Hungary in August 1991 marked the final turnaround in the country that had tried to change the political order by force in 1956. That revolution was brutally squashed by the Soviets. But this time, in the 1990-1991 revolution, the change was peaceful and successful.

Success did not happen overnight. Actually it started in 1960 with cautious contacts between the Holy See and the then communist government. This was primarily the work in those days of Cardinal Casaroli. His contacts and other contacts by Vatican officials in the 1960s and the '70s set the stage for the nonviolent change in power structure that occurred more than two decades later.

While their activities in the '60s and '70s were not coordinated, in many ways the United States and the Holy See were working along the same path. The U.S. was a longtime defender of the rights of Hungarian people to freedom of religion, human rights, and political pluralism. The unprecedented protection given to Cardinal Mindszenty at the American Embassy at Budapest from 1956 to 1971 and the U.S.-Vatican joint role in negotiating his flight from Hungary in 1971 were only two of the many signs of the cooperative U.S.-Vatican spirit to bring freedom to the Hungarian people.

One problem that frequently surfaced in discussions with Hungarian visitors to Rome in the 1991-92 period was the problem of Hungarian minorities in Slovakia and Romania. Here I would sometimes lose my patience as my Hungarian friends would frequently advocate that certain parts of Slovakia and Romania should be returned to Hungary because of the presence of Hungarian people living there. There was little thought of the duty of minorities in those two countries to accept their responsibilities as citizens.

This is part of the problems in that area of Europe, where the attachment to language and culture is so deep that it precludes the idea of a neutral citizen loyal to a constitution which will guarantee equal rights for everyone regardless of ethnic, religious, or racial background. This was also a touchy subject for the Holy See because these same groups would attempt to involve the Holy See on their side of the question. The Holy See actually embraced a position similar to that of the United States. There was general concurrence that it was the responsibility of the citizens living in a given country to be loyal to the constitution of that country. At the same time that country was expected to guarantee their rights as citizens and their ability to remain faithful to their culture and to their language.

Romania

Romania was a more difficult challenge to the Holy See than Poland, Czechoslovakia, and Hungary. The communist takeover after World War

II resulted in the abolishment of the 1920 concordat guaranteeing the rights of the Church. Nationalization of religious schools and passage in 1948 of a repressive anti-religious law which banned the Greek-rite Catholic Church and recognized only two Latin-rite dioceses. Diplomatic ties with the Holy See were severed in 1950.

The sweep of events in neighboring communist countries was also affecting Romania. The Holy See established contact in January 1990 with the National Salvation Front, Orthodox Patriarch Teoctist, and democratic leaders. These changes from communist oppression to freedom moved quickly, and on March 14, 1990, the Pope appointed seven Latin-rite and five Greek-rite bishops and thus reconstituted the entire Romanian Church hierarchy.

When the Romanian government indicated "surprise and concern" about the unilateral manner in which the Vatican made the appointments, the Holy See responded that it informs rather than consults government on the appointment of bishops. The Holy See is determined to protect its right to appoint bishops throughout the world without prior consultation with any of the governments concerned. The Vatican regards this as a fundamental aspect of religious freedom.

The change in Romania from communist oppression to democratic government is still incomplete. The local Catholic church leadership has spoken out on several occasions on the human-rights violations that have taken place since the overthrow of the communist dictatorship in 1989. The same concern for human-rights violations in the 1990-91 transition period was also expressed by the United States government.

Romania never had a tradition of parliamentary government or democratic institutions. It was ruled by an irresponsible monarch before World War II, and later Nazi sympathizers gained control of the government. This was followed by forty-five years of harsh communist rule.

The Orthodox Church leadership was compromised by too close an association with the Communist government. In the meantime, since the overthrow of the communist dictatorship in 1989, European and American Catholic organizations have been assisting Romanian Catholics to rebuild their churches, schools, and hospitals. This has increased the Orthodox Christians' suspicious and insecure attitude toward the Catholic leadership in Romania.

Followers of the Unitarian and Universalist Church in Romania were also abused during the communist rule. Unitarians and Catholics in the

Transylvanian part of Romania especially had a difficult time. Dr. William F. Schultz of the Unitarian and Universalist Church contacted me about the information that his organization had on the human-rights problems in Romania.

I was able to arrange for him to meet with Holy See officials concerned with these matters. This is a good example of two church groups that have vastly divergent theological positions cooperating together in the matter of human rights and religious freedom.

In 1990 I met with Archbishop Arapasu, Patriarch of the Romanian Orthodox Church. In a long conversation, he attempted to give me good reasons why the Orthodox Church cooperated with the communist leadership in the '60s, '70s, and '80s. When the subject of the Catholic Church came up, he was obviously suspicious that, given their worldwide connections, they would take advantage of their resources and promote their church to the disadvantage of the Orthodox Church. I discussed the Patriarch's suspicions with the Catholic Archbishop of Budapest, Iaon Robu, who was well aware of them. The Holy See was also aware of the suspicious attitudes and cautioned the Catholic leadership in Romania to move carefully.

Both the United States and the Holy See know that the lack of any democratic traditions, combined with the suspicious attitudes of the majority Romanian Orthodox Church toward the Hungarian minority community and the Catholic Church, could impede progress toward a society guaranteeing freedom of religion, human rights, and political pluralism. But progress has been made. This is their first attempt at democratic government, and the development of institutions is something that cannot be done overnight. Meanwhile, the constant vigilance of the United States, the Holy See, and others in regard to human rights and religious freedom guarantees that continued progress should be made in this country.

An indication that the human-rights situation had improved in the few years since the overthrow of communist control in 1989 was the visit in April 1993 of Romanian President Ion Iliescu with U.S. President Clinton. The meeting took place because the U.S. government was pleased with the progress taking place.

Bulgaria

Bulgaria had one of the strictest communist-atheist regimes when my wife and I visited the country in 1970. We could not find a Catholic church that was open. Freedom of religion and human rights were forbidden subjects for discussion.

Beginning in 1947, Catholic education and institutions were abolished, and the apostolic delegate was banished in 1949. All church activity was under state surveillance. No bishops were appointed until 1979, when the Pope was able to fill one vacant see. The attempted assassination of the Pope in 1981 put a further strain on Bulgarian-Holy See relations, as there was widespread belief that the Bulgarian intelligence agency was involved. This, however, did not restrain the Vatican from receiving the Bulgarian foreign minister on December 5, 1988. Two years later, on December 6, 1990, the Holy See established diplomatic relations with Bulgaria and sent a nuncio there in 1991.

There is now a strong commitment to religious freedom and human rights in Bulgaria. The 1991 elections were hailed by impartial observers as fair and just. The Pope has accepted an invitation to visit Bulgaria. He has also indicated little desire to reopen the investigation of the Bulgarian connection with his attempted assassination. While the Holy Father has not pushed the matter, the government of Bulgaria has reopened the files on the attempted assassination of the Pope and independent groups are reviewing them.

Albania

The role of the Holy See in the transformation of Albania from a severe communist government to a democratic one comes as a surprise to many because of the small number of Catholics in the country. The history of Albania is certainly bleak.

In 1967, the communist Albanian government, declaring that it had eliminated all religion in the country, proclaimed itself as the first atheist state in the world. Only small pockets of Catholics managed to survive clandestinely.

By 1990 the changes that had started in other parts of Eastern Europe began to have an impact on Albania. On November 4, the first open public Mass since 1967 was celebrated with four thousand Catholics in attendance. On November 11, at a second public Mass, over fifty thousand people attended.

The Saint Egidio community, an organization with strong ties to the Vatican, began in 1990 quietly giving assistance to the Albanian leaders. Vatican delegations visited the country on two occasions in 1991. On

December 31, 1991, the world's first atheist state became a secular state, and the new constitution guaranteed religious freedom to all religious groups.

The dramatic changes were also encouraged by the United States. Secretary of State James Baker visited Tirana on June 22, 1991, and hailed the Albanian acceptance of the religious freedom, human rights, and political pluralism. Here, as in other Eastern European countries, the sweep of change moved rapidly.

On February 1, 1993 Albanian Prime Minister Meksi, accompanied by Foreign Minister Serreke, met with the Pope. Prime Minister Meksi subsequently met with Cameron Hume, Embassy Deputy Chief of Mission, and told him that he had assured the Pope that his government was committed to the development of an open society with full respect for religious freedom. He also said that he wants Albania to be a country that has full respect for the rights of minorities.

On April 25 the Pope in a one day visit to Tirana was hailed for the support the Holy See gave in the Albanian transition from a communist dictatorship to democracy. The Holy See now has a nuncio in Tirana. Albanian leadership beginning in 1990 visited Rome and consulted with Catholic Church leaders. I met many of them visiting Catholic organizations in Rome. What a change in a state once officially atheistic!

The Former Soviet Union

Both the United States and the Holy See faced the same powerful opponent. The years following World War II (when the then Soviet Union acquired superpower status) were especially difficult for the United States and the Holy See. Both the United States and the Holy See were deeply involved — from 1945 to the late 1980s — in efforts to thwart the advance of atheistic communism. The struggle was carried on in different ways, but it continued as long as the Soviet Union was a superpower. The collapse of the Soviet Union started in the Reagan-Bush administration of 1980-1988 and was completed halfway through the first term of President Bush. Senior Vatican officials told me on several occasions that the world owed a great thanks to the United States for having orchestrated and played a leading role in this collapse and having done this in a non-violent way. When I left Washington in August 1989 to assume my duties in Rome, I knew that the U.S. government regarded the role of the Holy See as vital to any transformation that would take place.

With the arrival of Gorbachev on the scene in 1985, the Holy See sensed that the time was approaching when significant changes could take place. The Pope, who first referred to the one European community embracing both the Eastern and Western parts of Europe in 1979, repeated this prospect again on October 1, 1988, while addressing the European Parliament in Strasbourg.

The leading advisor to the Pope at this time was Cardinal Agostino Casaroli, Secretary of State and thus head of government at the Vatican. Cardinal Casaroli had pursued a decade's long "Ostpolitik" or policy of small steps and continuous contacts to keep the Church alive in the then U.S.S.R. and in Eastern Europe.

Dr. Henry Kissinger, former U.S. Secretary of State, reports that as a young professor he consulted in the 1960s with Cardinal Casaroli before making his first trip to Eastern Europe and the U.S.S.R. He told me that the Cardinal's advice was to practice "patience, perseverance, and patience."

This was the cornerstone of Vatican policy in the long period from the 1960s to the late 1980s. Once Gorbachev settled into power, results from the Vatican policy of staying in touch with Moscow became evident.

One of the first visible improvements in Holy See-U.S.S.R. relations occurred with the celebrations, in June 1988, for the millennium of Christianity in Russia, when the Vatican Secretary of State, Cardinal Casaroli, met in Moscow with President Gorbachev. This visit, Cardinal Casaroli later told me, was the one that encouraged him that Gorbachev was prepared to orchestrate significant changes in the Soviet Union that would result in greater human rights for the people. And the Cardinal felt assured that Gorbachev was committed to rapid and peaceful change.

Several months later, on October 6, the Pope flew over the U.S.S.R. on his way to a Eucharistic Congress in Seoul, Korea. This was the first time in twenty-five years of papal air travel that a pope had obtained permission from the Soviet government to fly over its territory.

The real turning point in U.S.S.R.-Holy See relations occurred on December 1, 1989, when Pope John Paul II received President Mikhail Gorbachev at the Vatican. As discussed in Chapter I, a profound sense of trust by the Pope toward Gorbachev developed at that meeting.

The two leaders discussed freedom of religion and human rights in the U.S.S.R. These same items were the center of the agenda when Boris Yeltsin, Russian Federation President, visited the Pope in December

1991. The dialogue started by Gorbachev rapidly evolved into an understanding that carried over to Yeltsin.

The drama of the Soviet Union collapse and the rise of the Russian Federation, the Ukraine, and other states from the former Soviet Union found the United States and the Holy See converging on most major policy issues affecting these countries. Their approaches varied, their methodology was different, but the goals usually converged.

During my last three years in Rome I had many contacts with Russian Envoy Jurij Karlov. He was a highly regarded member of the diplomatic corps. A very intelligent man, he had a long period of experience in Italy as the Vatican specialist in the Soviet Embassy to Italy. He knew Vatican traditions and spoke Italian very well. We exchanged pieces of information and even discussed strategies. One of the more emotional final luncheons in our honor occurred on February 16, 1993 when Jurij and his wife Tamara gave a luncheon honoring Margaret and me. We had developed a fine working relationship.

My wife, Margaret, and I visited Moscow in late December 1993. We were there two weeks before the visit of U.S. President Clinton. The goal of Russia's becoming a democratic state soon is a difficult one.

The Russian people have never had experience with democracy. The transition is complicated by the very difficult economic circumstances.

But both the United States and the Holy See know the importance of Russia to world peace. President Clinton, in his January 1994 visit, gave significant support to Yeltsin and his programs. The Holy See's policy has also been to back the democratic forces of Russia.

The convergences in U.S.-Holy See policies that occurred in Eastern Europe and in the former Soviet Union were not repeated as frequently in the Middle East. While both powers were major players, they had different policy positions. These will be discussed in Chapters VI and VII.

CHAPTER VI

Human Rights and Religious Freedom: Cornerstone of U.S.-Holy See Relations

ON MARCH 13, 1992, a senior diplomat of the Vatican Secretary of State telephoned me concerning the situation in Malawi. On the previous weekend the Catholic Bishops of this small country in southeastern Africa had issued a letter to all Catholics in the country reviewing the situation in Malawi on human rights, religious freedom, and political pluralism. The letter pointed out the weaknesses that existed and called upon the government to reform its policies and practices. The letter was a responsible statement of fact by an authoritative religious body within the country.

The reaction of the government of Malawi was violent. Threats were made by government officials that ranged from expulsion to execution. Malawi, a signatory of the U.N. charter on human rights, was presenting a clear and present challenge to the rights of religious groups to speak out on matters of vital concern to them.

The Holy See requested that the U.S. do whatever we could to assure that there was not any gross violations of human rights and religious freedom in Malawi. After reporting this matter to Washington, I met with Andrew Palmer, the British Ambassador to the Holy See, as Malawi is a member of the British Commonwealth. We met several times, and I kept in regular contact with the Holy See. The response from Washington was quick and strong. On April 29, 1992, the Assistant U.S. Secretary of State for African Affairs, Herman Cohen, met with Malawi Minister of State John Tempo. The Department of State officially reported on April 30 that Mr. Cohen

> "expressed deep concern over violations of human rights in Malawi, in particular the recent government actions against the Catholic Church over the Malawi Bishops' pastoral letter, the arrest and imprisonment of pro-democracy advocates — he called on the Malawi government to open up the political process, restore constitutionally guaranteed freedoms, and allow its citizens the right to freely criticize their government."

In my tenure as Ambassador, the cooperation between the Holy See and the United States on religious freedom and human rights matters was, as in the case of Malawi, the reason for my most frequent contact with Holy See officials.

This springs from a fundamental commitment. On January 1, 1992, in his World Day of Peace message, Pope John Paul II outlined the Vatican's human rights priorities as the "the right to life at every stage of development; the right to be respected regardless of race, sex or religious convictions; the right to material goods necessary for life, including the right to work in a fair distribution of its fruits for a well ordered and harmonious coexistence."

The Former Soviet Union

On December 1, 1989, Mikhail Gorbachev, then head of the Soviet Union, had an historic meeting with the Pope. Gorbachev was anxious to open wide the doors of dialogue with the world leader that his predecessors had so long vilified. When Gorbachev extended an invitation to him to visit the Soviet Union, the Holy Father set down requirements for his going; one was a guarantee by Moscow that human rights and religious freedoms would be enshrined in the laws of his country.

As Gorbachev subsequently said, Pope John Paul II played a decisive role in energizing the change in the old Soviet Union and in Eastern Europe from religious intolerance and human rights abuses to a full guarantee of religious freedom and human rights.

In this regard it should be noted that the Holy Father's concern for human rights is universal, not selective. He was not asking for guarantees only for Catholics, but he then and still campaigns for human rights and religious freedom for everyone.

Late in the evening of December 1, following the Vatican report to me of the Gorbachev-Pope meeting, I cabled the Department of State saying, "The Pope has stressed to Gorbachev the need for religious freedom in the U.S.S.R. for all religions." President Bush and James Baker had this report when they met a day later with Gorbachev.

The efforts of the Holy See to promote a change in the old Soviet Union and the Eastern European countries from oppression of human rights and religious oppression to states guaranteeing religious freedom and human rights coincided with the goals of the United States.

We cooperated fully in these efforts, and they were successful.

Cuba and Central America

In the case of Cuba, while we exchanged information and consulted one another, our efforts to influence a change in the oppressive Cuban regime had limited success. When I first arrived in Rome in August 1989, some were advocating a papal visit to Cuba as a way to stimulate a change. But the subsequent crackdown by Castro on human-rights activists led the U.S. to advise the Holy See that we felt a visit to Cuba was inopportune. Later in 1992, when the papal visit to the Dominican Republic was in the planning stage, the same possibility of a visit to Cuba was raised. Holy See officials again decided against such a visit, believing that it would not encourage an improvement in human rights for the Cuban people and could be misinterpreted in some quarters as support for Castro's brutal totalitarian regime.

On the other hand, in 1983 Pope John Paul II had gone to Nicaragua believing that such a visit would help the Nicaraguan people in their struggle against a regime violating human rights and religious freedom. The visit was a dangerous one for the Pope, but his concern for the human-rights issues overrode the personal security concerns. Modern communications made it possible for millions of people in the world to witness his strong statements condemning the human rights abuses of the government.

Seven years later in 1990 when the Nicaraguan people voted for a democratic government guaranteeing their freedom, there was joy in the leadership circles of both the United States and the Holy See. Another rigid, authoritarian communist government was replaced by a democratic one. Other problems, such as standard of living, did not disappear with the 1990 elections in Nicaragua, but communist oppression did.

South America

In May 1988, several weeks before the Pope left for a visit to Paraguay and Chile, I was still in private life. However, the International League for Human Rights contacted me about their concerns related to the violations of human rights of the Indian community in Paraguay. I transmitted the concerns of the League directly to Archbishop Pio Laghi, then Pronuncio in Washington, D.C.

I was very pleased to note that these concerns were included in a speech given by the Pope shortly after he arrived in Ascunción, Paraguay. He challenged the then Chief of State, General Alfredo Stroessner, to improve the human rights situation of the Indians, and within weeks of his visit improvements started to take place. The Pope was equally candid with the then President of Chile, General Augusto Pinochet Ugarte. Needless to say, I was pleased that my suggestions on what the Pope might say in Paraguay and Chile were accepted and used, even though they were sent only a few days before the Pope started his trip.

Consequently, there was little doubt in my mind when I arrived at my post in August 1989 about the human rights commitment of Pope John Paul II. And the experience in my years as Ambassador was that he is the champion of human rights for all. Not only is he committed, but he makes very effective use of the media to transmit his message.

Haiti: a Human Rights Nightmare

Haiti remained a human rights nightmare during my ambassadorial tour with the Holy See. There was a strong ray of hope in December 1990 that, with the election of the Reverend Jean Bertrand Aristide as President, the long tragic history of that country would change.

The election on December 16, 1990, was the first democratic presidential election in the country's history. President Aristide began with steps to improve the human-rights situation in Haiti. But within months conditions in Haiti began to deteriorate rapidly. Many of Aristide's followers, in demonstrations against opponents, contrary to the idea of improving human rights, used the violent practice of "Père Lebrun," which consist of placing a tire around the neck and shoulders of an opponent, igniting the tire, and letting it burn the person to death.

On September 29, 1991 President Aristide was overthrown by the military. Horrible human-rights abuses occurred in the weeks following the coup.

I was in contact with the Vatican Secretary of State on the Haitian tragedy. The United States held that since Aristide was elected in the first democratic election, he should be allowed to return. The U.S. was concerned about the human rights abuses that occurred during his administration but felt that priority should be given to returning the first democratically elected President to Haiti. The Holy See, on the other hand, viewed Aristide's record with alarm, especially his rhetoric and unpredictability, and consequently recognized the post-Aristide government of Haiti in 1992. Holy See officials told me that they felt it was imperative to encourage the government currently in place. They believed that the post-Aristide government was more likely to bring stability to the country. Holy See officials also pointed out to me that their primary interest in Haiti was the local people. They believed that being in contact with the existing government gave them greater influence.

Although this was not the policy of the U.S. government, I was not instructed to protest the Holy See's actions forcefully. My deputy chief of mission, Cameron Hume, reviewed our position with his counterparts at the Vatican.

As time passed in 1992 without a solution, the Haitian tragedy took on domestic U.S. implications. Aristide developed a large following in the Haitian communities within the United States. U.S. congressional hearings were the scene of emotional demonstrations by Aristide supporters from the Haitian communities.

The United States Catholic Conference in 1992 expressed disapproval of U.S. immigration policy that would not grant asylum to the Haitian refugees seeking admission to the United States. In the 1992 elections it became an issue of difference between the Bush Administration and Mr. Clinton, but there was no significant change in immigration policy toward Haiti once President Clinton was elected.

In late 1993, the Holy See let it be known that it would not oppose the peaceful return of Father Aristide to the Haitian presidency, in spite of a preference that priests not serve in secular office. (This surprised many, as Aristide had been violent in his rhetoric against the Pope and the Holy See.)

But the Clinton strategy toward that end, including embargo, blockade, and other sanctions, had not produced any notable increase of freedom and democracy for the terrorized Haitian people by the beginning of 1994.

Somalia, Liberia, and Sudan: Humanitarian Catastrophes in Africa

Civil strife, combined with natural disasters, created humanitarian catastrophes in Ethiopia, Chad, Somalia, Liberia, Mozambique, Sudan, and Angola while I was stationed in Rome. As the Ambassador of the United States, I worked with Holy See officials to obtain humanitarian relief and the end of the strife for the peoples in many African countries.

On July 30, 1992, I was called to the Vatican Secretariat of State by a senior official who expressed the concerns of the Holy See for Liberia. The Holy See turned to us because of the historic U.S. interest in that country. The prolonged civil strife in Liberia was of equal concern to the United States. Our mutual efforts brought relief supplies, but a political solution was difficult to find. Despite all our efforts, Liberia remained in a state of collapse for most of my tour of duty as Ambassador to the Holy See. On November 12, 1992, I participated in the memorial service for the five U.S. nuns killed by rebel forces in Liberia.

My wife and I had visited Liberia several times. Few would regard it as an inviting place to live. Those five sisters had volunteered for service to the poor people of Liberia. Hardly anyone knew their names. I gave one of the readings at the memorial Mass in Rome. Somehow I felt that more should have been said for those five American women who were brutally killed in an area where they had turned down suggestions that they return to Monrovia for greater security. They stayed with the people they had come to serve.

Margaret and I, as we were leaving the chapel at North American College, noticed a loneliness, an appearance of resignation among the sisters who attended the Mass. We felt so bad about it that we decided not to go into the city for a dinner party but to remain that evening at the residence. Mourning for the sisters was one reason for the bleak and lonely atmosphere in the chapel; another reason was Liberia itself. All the time I was in Rome, when a report came from Liberia, I hesitated a few seconds before reading it. All of the messages from that country in the 1989-1993 period brought news of starvation, chaos, and death.

During my tenure in Rome, efforts by the Holy See, the United States, and other countries could not end the ongoing Liberian tragedy.

Somalia

The situation in Somalia deteriorated so badly in early 1991 that the United States evacuated all government personnel from there. However, the U.S. government, through the Office of U.S. Foreign Disaster Assistance, provided medical and emergency food distribution in 1991 and '92. On January 23, 1992 the United States joined with other nations of the world at the United Nations Security Council which adopted Resolution 783 calling for an immediate cease-fire in Somalia.

However, for most of 1992 the U.N. resolution was ignored, and the situation rapidly deteriorated into chaos and anarchy. Through television, the human tragedy of thousands of children dying was brought into the homes of people throughout the world. On various occasions in 1992, the Pope spoke about the tragedy of Somalia. I would inform the department of the essential comments of what he had to say in each instance.

By December of 1992 it was clear that another Holocaust was in the making. Thanks to TV coverage, millions of people throughout the world saw the tragedy, reacted strongly against it, and pressured their governments to do something about it. The U.N. Security Council, in a unanimous vote, authorized the commitment of troops to Somalia to guarantee the safe distribution of humanitarian relief. The U.N.-authorized military activity was for clearly defined humanitarian purposes.

In December 1992, in the last days of his administration, President Bush cooperated with the United Nations and authorized the commitment of 28,000 troops to Somalia to clear the way for humanitarian relief. Our embassy discussed this development with Holy See officials. We felt this action was in response to worldwide revulsion at the ongoing tragedy of Somalia, where hundreds were dying each day. Ever since the 1990 expression of concern by the Holy See on the Somalian tragedy, we kept in contact with them on this matter. The U.S. resolution authorizing this military action was voted on December 3, 1992, and we reviewed the matter with Vatican officials the following morning.

Within twenty-four hours of the joint U.S.-U.N. action, Pope John Paul II gave a strong endorsement of the U.S. action in Somalia. He said that there was "an obligation to intervene" in this tragedy. In our subsequent talks with the Cardinal Angelo Sodano and Archbishop Jean-Louis Tauran, they applauded the leadership being given by the United States in this international humanitarian effort.

The Pope also said that "war and internal conflict condemn civilians to die" — and "in such situations food and medical assistance must be assured by removing all obstacles." The 1992 Somalia situation resulted in Pope John Paul's strongest and most explicit statement in support of the use of force to stop the killing of civilians and to assure that they had access to humanitarian supplies of food and medicines.

But in the spring and summer of 1993, as the Clinton administration proceeded to authorize U.S. troops to take military action against Somali warlords, the Holy See indicated its concern about the change of mission from aiding humanitarian assistance to engaging in military action.

The news in early 1994 on Somalia was indeed grim. President Clinton has announced that U.S. forces will be withdrawn in the spring of 1994. Other countries have announced similar intentions. The internal chaos of the country continues.

The community of nations needs to agree to a formula on when and how to intervene when, as Pope John Paul said, "there is an obligation to intervene." And once such a decision is made, there is an obligation to carry out the mandate.

Sudan

As the Pope was preparing to depart for the Dominican Republic in the first few days of October 1992, he met with the Bishops of Sudan. They brought him a very disturbing report on the expanding violations of human rights and religious freedom by the Sudanese government. The victims were primarily Christians and followers of traditional African religions. On October 9 I was summoned to the Vatican, along with Ambassadors from seven other European and African countries to meet with Archbishop Tauran, Secretary for Relations with States. We were told that the Pope was deeply distressed by these reports he had received from the Sudanese bishops.

We were requested to inform our governments that it was the Holy Father's request that our governments indicate strong objections to the violations of religious freedom and human rights in Sudan. The United States had already spoken very strongly against these abuses, and I was able to brief Archbishop Tauran and his colleagues on what the U.S. had done.

The Holy See had thus energized eight countries to take action or additional steps on this matter. We were also asked to strongly urge our governments toward increased efforts to supply relief assistance for the victims of the Sudanese government persecutions.

In his February 1993 trip to Africa, the Pope made a brief visit to Khartoum, the capital of Sudan. As soon as it was announced in late 1992 that Sudan would be included in the papal trip to Africa, there was opposition to it in some quarters of the United States Department of State. Some felt that the Pope's visit would be used by the Sudanese government as a sign of his approving what the government was doing. I cabled a strong approval of the planned visit, as I was sure that the Pope would seize the opportunity to set forth his message forcefully on human rights and religious freedom.

He did exactly that. Within minutes after his arrival on February 10, 1993, he met with Christian Sudanese leaders and others, assuring them of his strong support and concern for them. He told them they were not alone and that he and the Church would continue to campaign for their legitimate human rights. He then met with Sudanese government leaders, including General Omer Hassan Ahmed el-Bashir, and in precise clear language told them about their obligation to protect the human rights of all — including minority groups. In effect, he tongue-lashed the Sudanese leaders for the human-rights and religious-freedom abuses in their country. And thanks to modern communications, the world saw what happened. He communicated to the world that these violations were taking place and he expected the Sudanese government to mend its ways. The Pope's nine-hour visit was a dramatic success. He faced General Bashir and said that "minorities within a country have the right to exist with their own language, culture, and traditions, and the state is morally obliged to leave room for their identity and self-expression." Christians, the majority of them Catholic, represent only seven percent of Sudan's twenty-five million people. Within a brief time after departing from his plane, he said, "Rigorous respect for the right to religious freedom is a major source and foundation of peaceful coexistence." The Pope said this because he knew that thousands of refugees, many of them Christians, had fled from southern Sudan to camps outside of Khartoum, where they were subject to Islamic law. The bottom line of the Pope's position was that Islamic law must not be imposed upon Christians.

Economic assistance to Africa also remains very high on the list of papal priorities. In his 1990 visit to Tanzania, Pope John Paul II said, "Let the world not forget the urgent needs of the people of Africa. In the name of our common humanity, I appeal to the more developed nations of the earth to inaugurate a new era of solidarity with Africa based on justice and respect." The interest of the U.S. Embassy to the Holy See in the southern part of the African continent extended in 1992 to the neighboring countries of Zimbabwe and Zambia because of the very serious drought there.

Marilyn Quayle, wife of the then Vice President, after visiting several of the drought-stricken areas in Southern Africa, stopped in Rome for a brief visit. I gave a luncheon in her honor on May 23, 1992, so she could brief Vatican officials concerned with these matters. Her graphic up-to-date descriptions of the impending tragedy was appreciated by the Vatican officials responsible for relief activities.

Mozambique

On October 4, 1992, I attended the peace-signing ceremonies in Rome which ended the internal conflict in Mozambique. Starting in the 1980s, a civil war between the then Marxist government of Mozambique and a revolutionary movement had by 1992 taken over seven hundred thousand lives and ravaged the country.

It came to an end on October 3, following a unique 2½-year period of negotiations where the Saint Egidio Community, a Catholic organization with close ties to the Holy See, played a major role.

The Catholic Bishops of Mozambique, knowing the pain and distress that this conflict was causing the Mozambique people, approached the Saint Egidio leadership, which started the negotiations.

A multi-track process started, involving the governments of Zimbabwe, South Africa, Botswana, Tanzania, Kenya, Italy, Portugal, and the United States.

The unique aspect of these peace negotiations was that a non-state, the Saint Egidio community, was playing the role of discrete quarterback. Its influential role was enhanced by its very close connection to the Holy See. The U.S. government cooperated through its Embassy to the Holy See. Cameron Hume, Deputy Chief of Mission, was in almost daily contact with the participants. His role represented official U.S. interest and was frequently backed up by representatives from the Bureau of African Affairs of the U.S. Department of State. During this period the U.S. government, encouraged by the peace negotiations, increased its humanitarian aid to Mozambique. U.S. aid in various forms amounted to over $200 million yearly in this critical period.

Ending the conflict of Mozambique was the point of convergence for both the Holy See and the United States. During my tour of duty in Rome, I watched closely as this cooperation and cooperation with other states evolved into the peace-signing ceremonies of October 3, 1992.

The presence of Saint Egidio, the bishops of Mozambique, and the Holy See, along with the United States, gave a legitimacy to the process. Both President Chissano of Mozambique and the rebel leaders along with their families were received by the Pope in private audiences in the days following the October 1992 peace-signing.

I was pleased in early January 1993 to transmit to Cameron R. Hume the Superior Honor Award for his key role for the Mozambique peace negotiations. Shortly after the peace accord was signed the previous October, I had recommended this to the Department of State. There was overwhelming support for this award.

Zaire: a Question of Leadership

A sensitive situation developed over the role of the Catholic Church leaders in Africa. They frequently had superior leadership skills and the respect of many citizens in their respective countries. Foreign embassies, including the U.S., recognizing their leadership qualities would suggest that they should take on government leadership responsibilities.

Such recommendations were coming from Western embassies in Kenya, Central African Republic, Cameroon, Benin, and Zaire.

The situation in Zaire was the most troubling. Both the United States and the Holy See were concerned in the early 1990s about the approaching political and humanitarian disaster in Zaire.

Marshall Mobutu, the longtime dictator of Zaire, was a creation of the U.S. government. He came to power soon after the collapse of Belgian rule in the then Congo. His long rule deteriorated into a disastrous situation of poverty and governmental waste in the 1990s. The principal aid-donor countries, the United States, France, and Belgium, were searching for ways to provide for an orderly transition to a more democratic government.

A new leader was needed, and Archbishop Monsengwo Pasinya Laurent of the National Conference emerged as a leading candidate. An impressive man, the Archbishop quickly obtained the respect of American, Belgian, and French officials who visited Zaire.

As the situation worsened in late 1991 and in 1992, I received reports from the Department of State praising the Archbishop as a leader who had the confidence of most factions in Zaire. The National Conference was conceived as an instrument to bring about a peaceful transition to democracy. My Belgium and French colleague Ambassadors imparted the same high regard for the Archbishop.

As Archbishop Monsengwo prepared for a visit to Washington in late June 1992, I discussed the matter with Cardinal Tomko, who was in charge of Church activities throughout Africa and Asia.

Cardinal Tomko, while recognizing Monsengwo's brilliance and the need in Zaire for a new leader, told me that the Pope personally informed Monsengwo that he was prohibited by canon law from accepting any government position. I subsequently discussed the matter with Archbishop Tauran, and he repeated the same prohibition to me. Working closely with Cameron Hume and Deborah Graze, the political officer, I cabled the department pointing out the Vatican's regulations prohibiting priests and bishops from assuming government positions. I indicated that the Holy See was becoming uncomfortable with the prominent and increasingly autonomous political role of Archbishop Monsengwo.

I went on to recommend that the Monsengwo visit to the U.S. be used to highlight U.S. support for the work of the National Conference toward a transition government. I urged the department to avoid giving the appearance that there was high-level support for the Archbishop personally.

Monsengwo was well received in Washington, but both President Bush and Secretary James Baker were aware of my concerns and were low-key in their meetings with Monsengwo. I heard later that some officials in both the U.S. Embassy to Zaire and in Washington were not pleased with my "interference" with their opinion that Monsengwo should be the successor to Mobutu.

South Africa

A major concern for the Holy See in Africa while I served as Ambassador was the situation in South Africa. Apartheid was regarded with as much horror by the Holy See as it was by the United States. As the South African leadership in 1990-1991 seemed to be embarking on major changes in their policy toward the African, "Coloured," and Asian communities, the Holy See sent Cardinal Roger Etchegaray on a special mission in mid-1991 to study the situation.

Working on South African matters with the Holy See brought back memories that my wife and I share resulting from our 1962 visit there. We were the guests in Durban of then Archbishop Dennis Hurley. He had invited Catholic leaders from the white, black, Asian, and "coloured" communities to meet us at his home for dinner. He also arranged for us to meet Nobel Prize Laureate Albert Luthuli secretly at a priest's home.

Several years later when I wanted to return to the Republic of South Africa, I was refused a visa. I learned that I was a prohibited alien. As a result of having dined with Catholic leaders at the home of Archbishop Hurley and meeting Albert Luthuli, the South African government indicated that I was either a communist "dupe" or a fool.

The thirty years between my visit there and my arrival in Rome had brought many changes to South Africa. I found the mood at the Vatican cautiously hopeful and decided to explore the situation in South Africa more thoroughly.

On July 25, 1991, I met with Cardinal Etchegaray, who heads the Council for Justice and Peace. While he felt that "irreversible progress had taken place," it was still not the "right time" for the Holy See to respond positively to the South African government's request for diplomatic relations. Previously, Nelson Mandela, head of the African National Congress, had visited the Holy Father. Vatican officials reported to me that there had been a positive reaction to his commitment to obtain human rights and justice for all in South Africa.

Indonesia and Timor

One of the first trips overseas that Pope Paul II made after my arrival in the summer of 1989 was his October visit to Indonesia. With Catholics only numbering around six million, or 3.5% of the population of around 180 million, the Pope was faced with the challenge of religious freedom in a country where an Islamic majority in Indonesia had not been friendly to the Catholic majority on the island of Timor.

On October 9, 1989, Pope John Paul II arrived in Jakarta. His address at the state reception pressed for human rights and self-determination while also applauding achievements in building a pluralistic and tolerant society. "At times," the Pope noted, "nations are tempted to disregard fundamental human rights in a misguided search for political unity based on military or economic power alone."

During his five-day visit, the Pope emphasized individual Catholics' responsibility to society but also the state's obligations toward its citizens, including respect for human rights. Repeated themes during the visit included Indonesia's religious and cultural diversity, the challenge of building and maintaining harmony there, and the "Pancasila" state ideology toward these ends. In his sermon, John Paul recognized a power in Indonesian nationalism that reinforces the traditional religious tolerance of the Indies. Following his visit in Jakarta, he went to East Timor. The Pope thus was the first world leader to visit East Timor since its integration with Indonesia in 1976.

While noting the essential need for Indonesian, Muslim, Catholic, Buddhist, and Hindu communities to enter into dialogue and communication, the Pope's homily in East Timor explicitly addressed the temporal problems of hatred and death which befell the people there. He spoke frankly about the problems and said that respect for the rights that render life more fully human must be firmly insured.

Despite a small scuffle in Dili, on the island of Timor, by twenty nationalist students, the Pope's visit to the world's most populist Islamic country was characterized by a warm and enthusiastic welcome by the diverse groups in Indonesia.

In an October 1991 visit for talks between the Indonesian minister of religion and the Holy See's head of government, Cardinal Sodano, the Vatican indicated that there was no major disagreement on the issue of religious freedom and fundamental human rights. The Pope subsequently praised Indonesia as a country with an Islamic majority that respects the rights of minority religions. In November 1991, when violence again occurred in East Timor, the Vatican assumed at first that it was a tragic human error. Later, when questions arose about the firmness of the government of Indonesia in determining who was responsible, the Vatican issued a strong statement reaffirming the right of Timor inhabitants to social peace and fundamental liberties.

Within a few months, the human rights and religious freedom problems in East Timor had improved. The Holy See was a major factor in the international pressure on Indonesia to improve the situation in East Timor. For example, on December 7, 1991, when accepting the credentials of the Indonesian Ambassador the Pope said:

> "In her recent history, Indonesia, too, has had do face situations of a painful and complex nature which show how difficult it can be to find that dynamic balance which would ensure the just protection of the overall interest of the nation and the fundamental rights of individuals and peoples."

When I departed Rome in 1993, the basic Vatican attitude was to remain alert to the possibility of human rights abuses occurring again in

East Timor. The same vigilance is being carried out by the U.S. government.

The Middle East

In the early 1990s, the Holy See was focusing on the absence of religious freedom in a few Islamic states. In his 1991 World Peace Day message, the Pope began by saying, "If you want peace, respect the conscience of every person," and then added that "extremely sensitive situations arise when a specifically religious norm becomes, or tends to become, the law of the state without due consideration for the distinction between the domains proper to religion and to political society."

The widely held belief that this aspect of his 1991 message was aimed at Saudi Arabia was confirmed in my subsequent meetings with senior Vatican officials.

Earlier, in his January 1990 message, the Pope had by inference referred to Islamic repression of Christians. It was evident that he was targeting Muslim-majority states when he said that "certain countries and certain religious majorities do not allow minorities to practice their faith — or even actively and legally participate in the political, social, and cultural progress of the nations of which they are members." Again, Holy See officials told me that the prime example of this violation of religious freedom was Saudi Arabia.

Israel

Concern of the Holy See for human rights abuses also extended to Israel. On October 10, 1990, the Pope condemned the violence that had occurred in the preceding days in Jerusalem. He also denounced the "unjust" situation in the occupied territories.

On the same day, L'Osservatore Romano published on page one an editorial condemning "the brutal violence perpetuated against persons who, furthermore, find themselves offended even in their most natural right."

The very strong editorial went on to deplore "acts against man and against peace which call for the foremost condemnation."

Holy See officials indicated to me their belief that the Arab people living in Israel, and certainly those in the occupied territories, were disadvantaged. This inequitable situation in their opinion would continue until there was an overall Middle East peace settlement. As will be discussed in the next chapter, this is why the Vatican hailed the Middle East peace negotiations initiated in 1991 in Madrid.

China

Both the Holy See and the United States were confronted by the same human-rights and religious-freedom concerns in China. While there was a belief in both Washington and the Vatican that keeping the door open for communications would bring about some changes in the long run, the Tiananmen Square disaster of 1989 raised serious concerns with both parties.

When I arranged for the meeting of Secretary Baker with Cardinal Angelo Sodano on November 8, 1991, the promotion of human rights and religious freedom in China was on the agenda.

This was the first meeting of Cardinal Sodano, first with Secretary Baker, then with President Bush. Born in northern Italy, Sodano had entered the career diplomatic service of the Holy See as a young priest and rose systematically through the ranks. His last overseas post was as nuncio to Chile. Named Secretary of State in 1990 to succeed Cardinal Casaroli, after serving as de facto foreign minister, he became a Cardinal in June 1991.

Cardinal Sodano came from the heart of the Italian Catholic Church establishment and was able to give the Pope valuable insights into both the Italian Church and government politics.

The exchange with Secretary Baker focused on how to accelerate the process of change in China that could reduce the current abuses. Cardinal Sodano brought up the matter of the right of the Catholic Church to carry out its mission in China. He and Archbishop Tauran, Secretary for Relations with States, reported on the bishops who were imprisoned or under house arrest. Secretary Baker, who would be visiting Beijing a few days later, asked the Vatican to give me a list of the imprisoned bishops which I would cable to him, and he would then raise the matter with Chinese government officials.

I did this several days later, and the results were gratifying. Several bishops were released either from prison or from house arrest. The United States was helpful in other ways through assuring that bishops, priests, and seminarians had the basic freedoms to carry out their missions. Seminarians from China were thus able, in 1991 and 1992, to come to the United States for their theological studies.

My China experience was a sometimes frustrating one. Having been active in human rights organizations before assuming my duties in Rome, I was approached by a longtime former colleague who sincerely felt that the Holy See and the United States were too timid in their attempts to improve the human-rights situation in China.

I knew that both parties were carrying out the complicated task of promoting human rights in China. The United States was doing it within the framework of continuing discussions with the Beijing government. Since the Holy See had no official presence in Beijing, their efforts had to be more indirect. The efforts of the United States and the Holy See can be backed up by continuing international news coverage of human-rights and religious-freedom abuses in China when they occur.

Vietnam

Both the United States and the Holy See were interested in achieving some improvement in the human-rights and religious-freedom situation in Vietnam.

Cameron Hume and I met with Monsignor Claudio Celli, who was then the point man of the Vatican on their project to open the Asian communist societies to activities of the Catholic Church. He had made several trips to Vietnam, and we exchanged information, discussing strategy on how to achieve at least minimum human rights and religious-freedom goals in Vietnam.

The situation for Catholics in Vietnam remains difficult. Everything the Church wants to do needs the prior approval of the government. And approval is not now normally given. Seminaries, for example, may admit student only once every three years, and then the government claims that it has the authority to grant or withhold approval of each individual applicant.

The Vietnamese government continues to demand the right of approving all candidates for ordination. And the government demands the right to approve the assignment of all priests.

The Holy See found that the government of Vietnam wanted Church personnel for their schools, but only under their own limited conditions. Vatican officials resisted such requests but continued the dialogue — with very little success.

One complicating factor for the Holy See was the situation of the Archbishop of Saigon, Nguyen Van Thuân. After a very brief stay in

Vietnam in 1991 he was asked by the government to leave and return to Rome.

Vietnamese authorities have charged that Archbishop Thuân was a U.S. government agent. No evidence was ever offered to support this allegation. Vietnamese suspicions seem basically rooted in the fact that he is a nephew of the late Vietnamese President Ngo Dinh Diem. The President of Vietnam was close to the U.S. government. He was assassinated in 1963.

I met with Archbishop Thuân on several occasions in Rome after he returned there in 1991. An energetic, articulate leader, he was also popular with the people. I believe that this was one reason why the Holy See wanted him in the key position of Archbishop of Saigon and why the government of Vietnam did not want him there.

French President François Mitterrand visited Vietnam in February 1993. Both the Holy See and the United States thought that his visit would assist in encouraging dialogue and contacts. Suggestions have been made that both the United States and the Holy See should establish diplomatic ties with Vietnam. Many obstacles remain before this can be accomplished. Meanwhile, both powers are exchanging information and strategies on how to bring Vietnam into the family of nations that respect human rights and religious freedom.

The worldwide nature of both the U.S. and Vatican's domains will frequently offer opportunities for cooperation. Coordinating the exchange of information and strategy on these matters was one of my principle responsibilities while serving as Ambassador. Numerous opportunities will exist in the future for cooperation on human-rights and religious-freedom matters to continue and to expand. Agreement on goals will not always lead to agreement on means to obtain those goals.

CHAPTER VII

The United States and the Holy See on the Gulf War: Divergent Positions

L ATE IN THE afternoon on January 16, 1991, I received an urgent cable at the embassy containing the response of President Bush to the Pope's plea that the United States not initiate war against Saddam Hussein to solve the problem of Iraq's takeover of Kuwait. I was instructed to deliver the letter to the highest Vatican official available that evening. I knew the reason why: The bombing would start the next day, and the United States wanted the Pope to have the President's letter before the bombing started. I followed my instructions. It was a difficult time for me. I knew what my duty was, but I was torn inside about the expansion of the war.

The Vatican Deputy Foreign Minister, Monsignor Claudio Celli, was waiting for me on the steps to the papal apartments. I knew that war was imminent. My mood was quiet and somber. I believe he knew that war was also going to happen, but under diplomatic courtesies and procedures, we would not discuss it. I gave him the letter from the President, saying it was urgent that he give it immediately to the Holy Father. He said he would do that and the Holy Father would have it within the next few minutes. I said good-bye. There was not much else that I could say. I left quietly and proceeded immediately to the Saint Damas courtyard, where my car was waiting for me.

As we were winding our way through the ancient streets of the Vatican, I wanted to stop at Saint Anne's Church within the Vatican walls. I felt that I needed to be alone for a few moments for prayer and reflection on what was going on, but as we approached the church I decided not to stop there because my bodyguards were right outside the walls waiting for me and they would notice that I entered the church. I was fearful that they would come to the conclusion that the war would start soon. The bodyguards were always with me. That afternoon Antonio, who had been assigned to me since my arrival in Rome, asked me why I seemed so sad. Many months later he told me that he "knew why."

I therefore told Claudio to proceed quickly to the residence. Arriving a few minutes later I told my wife that war was imminent. I also told her about the circumstances of my visit at the Vatican; that I had delivered the response from the President. It was still early evening. We had dinner alone. It was really difficult to eat and also difficult to carry on a conversation. It was a long and somber evening. I worked on some papers but accomplished little. Around midnight, I took my first sleeping pill in years. We prayed together that God's will would be done. Several hours later, a telephone call from Washington informed us that the air attack had started. It had been evident for weeks that the Pope was very uncomfortable with the possibility that there would be an all-out military attack on Iraq. In his letter to the President, which I had transmitted by immediate cable on January 15 after telephoning the contents, the Pope "stressed the tragic consequences which a war in the area would have." He went on to say that it was his "firm belief that war is not likely to bring an adequate solution to international problems."

The President's reply came within twenty-four hours. His letter said that "since Iraq's invasion of Kuwait on August 2, acts of aggression have been visited daily on victims of this war waged by Iraq. The international community has sought relentlessly to reverse this crime and establish a true peace. Our aim is not only peace in the Gulf region but a peaceful world built on the foundations of morality." He went on to say "the world community stands ready to respond — should I say, demonstrate its willingness to comply in full with the resolutions of the U.N. Security Council."

The Convergences and the Differences

Several days previously, on January 13, at a public prayer service, Pope John Paul II had called for both an Iraqi pullout from Kuwait and the convocation of a peace conference in the Middle East. He wanted independence to be restored to Kuwait but was opposed to the use of military force to accomplish this. The day before, in an address to the entire diplomatic corps, he had unequivocally condemned Iraq's invasion of Kuwait but said recourse to war would represent a "decline" for humanity.

Most of my professional life was dedicated to dialogue, persuasion, and advocacy. I disliked violence with a passion, having seen the worst of it in Burundi and Uganda, where I had served as U.S. Ambassador. And now it was at my doorstep. I knew all the facts of Iraq's cruel invasion

Ambassador and Mrs. Thomas Patrick Melady with Pope John Paul II during presentation of credentials in private audience, October 1, 1989 (see Preface).

Top: Soviet President Mikhail Gorbachev at early audience with Pope John Paul II in private papal library in the Vatican, December 1989 (see Chapter I). Bottom: Cardinal Casaroli in the Oval Office of the White House, Washington, D.C., with President George Bush and Ambassador Melady, October 1990.

Top: DEA agents hold Panama's General Manuel Noriega in custody aboard a C-130 jet shortly after Noriega surrendered to U.S. authorities in January 1990. Bottom: Gorbachev and Pope John Paul meet again in a more cordial mood to discuss religious liberty in the Soviet Union, November 1990 (see Chapter I).

Perpendicular: Pope Paul VI addresses the United Nations General Assembly, New York, making an historic plea for peace on October 4, 1965 (see Chapter II).

Nineteenth-century U.S. diplomatic representatives to the Papal States: (from top) John P. Stockton, 1858-1861; Alexander W. Randell, 1861-1862; and Rufus King, 1863-1867 (see Chapter III).

General Mark Clark, unsuccessfully nominated as United States Ambassador to the Vatican by President Harry S Truman in 1951 (see Chapter III).

Personal representatives of U.S. Presidents to the Pope (clockwise from upper left): Myron Taylor, Henry Cabot Lodge, David Walters, Robert F. Wagner.

Photo from Mrs. Wagner

Ambassadors to the Holy See (clockwise from upper left): William A. Wilson, 1984-1986 (special rep., 1980-1984); Frank Shakespeare, 1987-1989; Thomas Patrick Melady, 1989-1993; and Raymond L. Flynn, 1993- (see Chapter IV).

State Department

First Nuncio of the Holy See to the United States, Cardinal Pio Laghi.

Perpendicular: President and Mrs. George Bush and Secretary and Mrs. James Baker flank Pope John Paul II, with Ambassador and Mrs. Melady at left, in the Pope's private library at the Vatican (see Chapter VII).

Felici Photo

Cardinal Angelo Sodano, Papal Secretary of State during Ambassador Melady's tenure at the Vatican (see Chapter VII et passim).

Archbishop Jean-Louis Tauran, who served as the Vatican's Substitute
Secretary of State for Relations with Other States (see Chapter VII).

Top: Cardinal John J. O'Connor of New York, a major player in diplomatic recognition of Israel (Chapter VIII). Bottom: Republics of Ex-Yugoslavia (IX).

Nine thousand disabled, most more than this, struggled to attend the Vatican Health-Care Conference on the Disabled in November 1992 (see Chapter XI).

John Zierten

Cardinal Roger Etchegaray of France managed several offices of the Curia involved with diplomatic and humanitarian concerns (see Chapter XI).
L'Osservatore Romano Photo

Two U.S. cardinals serving as members of the Curia: (above) Cardinal William Wakefield Baum, Major Penitentiary; (below) Cardinal Edmund Casimir Szoka, president of the Prefecture for the Economic Affairs of the Holy See.

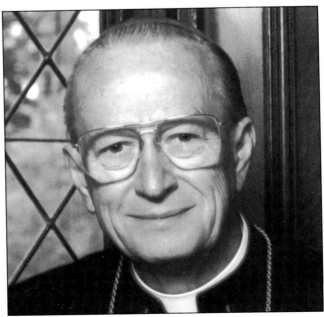

and occupation of Kuwait. I prayed that a solution would be found that did not require going to war against Iraq.

But as we approached January 15, I sensed the inevitable. And furthermore, I was an Ambassador, sworn to "defend" U.S. interests as determined by the President.

For several weeks before this, I realized that in all probability the President would initiate the military action authorized by the United Nations. I had studied the just-war theories as a university student. I knew that it was a disputed subject in Catholic intellectual circles. However, after some research I cabled the President on January 11 and said, "For some time the 'Just War' teaching was a part of Catholic doctrine" which now has evolved into the "Just Use of Force" doctrine. I said that the Gulf War situation could meet the six criteria for a "Just War" and suggested that the President use this in explaining why force could be justified after January 15. As a former professor of political science, I had discussed with past students the criteria for a Just War. Relying on that background, my cable said:

1. *Just Cause*
Iraq committed aggression against a small neighbor. It was brutalizing the people of Kuwait.

2. *Competent Authority*
The competent authority that authorized the use of force was the United Nations. Thanks to modern communications, the debate at the U.N. was adjudicated by the people throughout the world — the meetings were not in secret; the issues were publicly discussed.

3. *Just Intent*
The just intent, I pointed out, was set forth in the U.N. Resolution: freeing the people of Kuwait and restoring that country to the independent family of nations.

4. *Last Resort*
There had been an unprecedented exploration of all peaceful alternatives to accomplish the U.N. goal of obtaining freedom for Kuwait.

5. *Probability of Success*
There was every evidence that the use of force would be quick and successful.

6. *Proportionality*
The use of force and its subsequent cost would be in proportion to the good accomplished.

The Problem: the Fifth and Sixth Criteria

It was the fifth and sixth criteria where the Holy See and the United States differed. There was a clear, overriding fear on the part of the Holy See that the use of the military force to free Kuwait would cause a regional conflict that would match the suffering in the Vietnam War. Furthermore, I was told by a senior Holy See official that "war is never justified unless every other means to resolve the conflict has been exhausted."

As soon as the hostilities started, my security coverage was greatly expanded. The U.S. and Italian governments were greatly concerned about presumed terrorists in Italy. We had security protection from the first day of our arrival. Margaret and I soon learned to live with it.

The relatively short period of hostilities established that the United States and the United Nations leaders had been correct in their assessment that it would be a very brief conflict. But the central fact was that the Pope was not pleased with the use of war to resolve this crisis. Several weeks earlier he had said that "war is an adventure with no return." In the months preceding the January 15 deadline, there were many demonstrations in Italy against the pending U.N. action. And generally the Pope's anti-war statements were quoted.

On January 12, after his meeting with the diplomatic corps, the Pope came up to me and said he was "thinking of President Bush." He said that he understood the President had a difficult decision to make but that he was confident that he would make "the right decision." I immediately transmitted this message to Washington. There was no doubt in my mind that by the "right decision," the Pope wanted the United States to avoid the use of war.

Not Pacifist at Any Cost

As the Pope spoke against the use of military force to free Kuwait, pacifist and leftist groups took the Pope's comments out of context to use as their rallying cry. I called this to the attention of both Cardinal Sodano and Archbishop Tauran. I was subsequently able to report that on February 17, 1991 the Pope said in a radio broadcast that "we are not pacifist at any cost. . . . We desire peace and justice, to be instruments of peace. There can be no peace without justice, and justice comes from love and charity." In December 1990, the U.S. was under strong editorial attack in various newspapers and journals in Italy. The two that were most vicious were *Sabato (Saturday)* and *Trente Giorni (Thirty Days)*. They were more severe than the communist newspaper. These two publications did have Italian Catholic connections, but when wire services in Europe and the United States would report their editorial comments they would indicate that they were reports coming from the Vatican. The most violent of the attacks on the United States occurred in *Sabato*, which proclaimed that President Bush should receive the Nobel Prize for war. I received many expressions of outrage from Americans when this appeared. I took up the matter of these two publications with Vatican officials, who assured me that they were not only not connected with the Vatican but that actually Vatican authorities had serious reservations about the editorial policies. On the other hand, rather strong criticism of U.S. actions in Iraq were also occurring editorially in *Civiltà Cattolica*. This is a distinguished Jesuit publication, and it was frequently reported that nothing would appear in the journal if it did not at least carry the silent consent of Vatican officials. It was difficult for me to honestly state to the Department of State that this journal did not reflect, in some way or another, Vatican opinion.

Two unsigned editorials highly critical of the U.S. that appeared in *L'Osservatore Romano*, the unofficial but yet so very official daily newspaper of the Vatican, were difficult to explain to Washington. Since I needed to make an evaluation of the articles in *Civiltà Cattolica* and *L'Osservatore Romano*, I consulted with my good friend Emanuele Scammacca, Italian Ambassador to the Holy See. I consequently informed Washington that the comments in these two publications frequently reflect Vatican thinking and that in these cases there was most likely a connection between the articles and the Vatican.

Catholic editorial comment in the United States was far less negative about the U.S. action in Iraq than it was in Italy. This probably was caused by the fact that there was not a united position by the United States Catholic bishops. I was in contact with U.S. Catholic Church leaders during this period. While I knew that my instructions came from the President and the Secretary of State, I also realized that President Bush was in respectful contact with several U.S. Catholic Church leaders. In the weeks leading up to the opening of hostilities in January, he had talked with Cardinals Bernard Law of Boston and John O'Connor of New York. These contacts were his usual ones, as neither he nor the White House staff maintained any regular, significant contact with the U.S. Catholic Conference. (Archbishop Daniel Pilarczyk of Cincinnati was President of the Conference at the time of the Gulf War.)

Cardinal Law was regarded as being sympathetic to the claim of President Bush that the Gulf War met the just-war criteria. He said that prayers for peace are "not fulfilled at the price of granting tyrants and aggressors an open field to achieve unjust ends." Cardinal O'Connor, on the other hand, seemed more concerned about the dangers of the war.

The strong opposition of the Holy Father to the Gulf War did present something of a dilemma to the U.S. Catholic leadership. But as one Cardinal told me, this was not a matter of faith and morals, and it was possible for a Catholic churchman to differ with the Pope on the Gulf War.

The other two large religious communities in the United States were clear on their approach to the war. The National Council of Churches was strong in opposition and the American Jewish Community was generally supportive of President Bush.

The attitudes and opinions of my colleagues in the diplomatic corps accredited to the Holy See varied greatly in those days. The Western European diplomats were sympathetic to our position. My Russian colleague, Jurij Karlov, refrained from any criticism! However, my Latin American colleagues generally joined the Ambassador of Cuba in criticizing the imperialistic action of the United Nations led by the United States.

The Italian Catholic left was probably the most emotional. Somehow they saw a vast U.S. plot allied with Israel to defeat Islamic independence movements. Because of the extra-heavy security protection I had during the Gulf War, I had little opportunity to converse with the average Italians that I would casually meet in the streets of Rome on this matter. But I doubt that they were as strongly opposed to the Gulf War as the Italian Catholic left.

Ground Offensive

The ground offensive started on February 23, and the President announced the cessation of hostilities on February 27. As it became apparent that the war was coming to a quick end, and that those who convinced Holy See officials that the war would last for years and become a quagmire like Vietnam were wrong, there was no change in the Holy See position. In the opinion of the Holy See officials, the decision to go to war in this instance was an error. Their position never changed. They still believe that it was a mistake.

On March 4 and 5 (1991), a conference on the Middle East took place, called by the Pope. The focus was the postwar situation in the Middle East. Attending were Catholic leaders from the Middle East, heads of humanitarian agencies, and the head of the United States Conference of Bishops. The Pope called for "peace in the region, interreligious dialogue, and solidarity." He also called for solutions to the problems in Lebanon and Palestine.

The Pope's concern about the overall problems in the Middle East area included, in addition to Lebanon and Israel, the future of the Palestinian people and the lack of religious freedom in Saudi Arabia. The Pope also mentioned the problem of religious freedom in Saudi Arabia when President Bush phoned him on March 8, 1991. I learned later that the President was disappointed in his phone conversation with the Pope. He felt that the conversation was "fractured," i.e., ill-understood. I felt bad about it, as I had recommended that he telephone the Pope. It was most likely a matter of accent which the telephone can magnify. When the President phoned the Pope following his 1992 operation, I cautioned him to restrict the conversation to social amenities.

No Action Against Saddam Hussein

I noticed in the days following the end of hostilities in the Gulf War that no action was being taken on my recommendation that Saddam Hussein be indicted as an international criminal. On January 18, 1991, I had urged the Department of State to initiate legal proceedings for an indictment against Saddam Hussein as a war criminal. In my message to the Department of State, I said, "Saddam Hussein is a tyrannical despot who has committed gross violations against humanity. The precedent established following World War II was that heads and leaders of government who commit crimes against humanity are subject to international law. To maintain that consistency of our action under international law, Saddam Hussein should be indicted."

I felt strongly about the proposal, as I was the last U.S. Ambassador accredited to Idi Amin in Uganda. I saw the brutality of his regime and recommended the closing of the U.S. Embassy in 1973, as I believed that a practicing brutal tyrant should not be dignified by the presence of a U.S. mission at the ambassadorial level. Following that, my wife, daughters, and I returned to the U.S., where I resumed my academic career.

In 1978, after my wife and I obtained all the documentation necessary for our book *Idi Amin: Hitler in Africa*, I, in a communication to President Carter, urged him to instruct the Attorney General of the United States to indict Idi Amin as a war criminal. Through the efforts of my good friend Leonard Schine, a trustee at Sacred Heart University, where I was then president, an appointment was arranged for my wife and me to meet with President Carter to discuss our recommendation. We went to Washington. Late in the evening of our arrival we received word that the appointment had been canceled. I was told that the matter was referred to Andrew Young, then U.S. Ambassador to the United Nations. I saw Mr. Young at a subsequent meeting, and nothing ever came of our request to indict Idi Amin.

The atrocities in Uganda continued, and my wife and I pressed on. Again through the good offices of the late Leonard Schine, we later had an appointment with United States Senator Frank Church of Idaho, chairman of the Senate Foreign Relations Committee. He was very busy and saw us when he took a break of a few minutes from a busy session in the U.S. Senate. We were told that he only had five minutes for us. My wife told him about a personal experience with some of the atrocities. Senator Church was obviously moved. He invited us to see him later that evening. We went into more detail on the atrocities in Uganda. At the end of the meeting, he agreed to sponsor legislation whereby the United States would have an embargo on the purchase of Ugandan coffee. My wife and I had researched the fact that the American dollar income from the purchase of Ugandan coffee was all going into the special fund for Idi Amin, which he used to pay for his terrorist forces. For the first time in the history of the United States, an embargo was passed by the Senate. Normally embargoes were the result of a presidential executive order. It played a major role in the collapse of the Idi Amin dictatorship in 1979.

Every time President Bush referred to Saddam Hussein as a war criminal, I thought of my experience with Idi Amin. That dictator was never formally charged for his crimes against humanity. He is now living comfortably in exile in Saudi Arabia.

I did not want this to happen to the dictator of Iraq. I assumed that the United States would proceed to indict Saddam Hussein when hostilities ended. This did not happen, and I was never briefed on why it was not done. This was one regret that I had on the outcome of the Gulf War. The people in Kuwait and Iraq who were killed and injured are owed an explanation as to why the man who was responsible for the horrible events was never indicted.

War Versus Police Action

Another regret that I had for the Gulf War period is that the United States and the United Nations did not develop a concept of police action rather than war.

I had urged in the fall of 1990 that the United States avoid using the term "war." Since every society has a police force, including Vatican City, I suggested in a cable to the Department of State on December 7, 1990, that the project be described as an international police effort to free Kuwait from the takeover by Saddam Hussein.

The persistent use of the word "war," rather than a police action by a proper authority (the United Nations), complicated my efforts to influence the Holy See to support — or at least not condemn — our activities in the Gulf War. In my conversations with Vatican officials, I would talk in the framework of a responsible authority taking police action to bring about a legitimate goal: in this case, the freeing of Kuwait. I was not very convincing, because all the news reports coming out of Washington talked about war. However, I understood the complications.

The United States Constitution requires the President to obtain Senate approval for initiating an action like the one contemplated against Iraq. Given both the U.S. Constitution and the worldwide buildup of military forces numbering more than half a million, it was politically not realistic, to describe the operation as a police action. In any event, as we approached the January 15, 1991, deadline, I knew that there would be opposition from the Holy See for any war action against Iraq. A lower-profile U.N. police action might have received a "no opposition" stand from the Holy See. But the U.S. Constitution and the extraordinarily large force put together for the military operations made this impossible.

Catholic Leader in Iraq

A sensitive matter for me during the Gulf War was the position of Raphael I Bidawid, Patriarch of the Chaldean Church of Iraq. Patriarch Bidawid, as head of the more than 300,000-member Chaldean Church, was the leading Catholic Church leader in Iraq, as the Chaldean Church is in communion with the Roman Catholic Church.

During the Gulf War, the Patriarch was an outspoken supporter of Saddam Hussein and an apologist for Iraq's aggression against Kuwait. He was frequently in Rome in the fall of 1990. On one occasion he described Saddam Hussein as "a real gentleman." On another occasion he said that the press was "in the pay of Israel and the United States."

I would be asked about what he said by the media in Rome. I would point out that the Vatican had consistently called for Iraqi withdrawal from Kuwait and denounced Iraqi missile attacks against population centers in Saudi Arabia and Israel. I was accredited to the Holy See as U.S. Ambassador and could avoid commenting on the statements of religious leaders from other countries.

However, from a personal point of view, I found it embarrassing that a Catholic Church leader would so openly associate himself with such a notorious and brutal tyrant as Saddam Hussein. While I did not speak publicly about these concerns concerning Patriarch Bidawid, I did express them privately to Archbishop Tauran and to my own U.S. Department of State colleagues.

End of the Gulf War Activities

The Gulf War hostilities came to an end on February 27, 1991. There never was a difficult time for me as the U.S. Ambassador to the Holy See during this war period as far as the attitude of Vatican officials toward me was concerned. I always presented the point of view of the U.S. government, which was my responsibility. They listened to me politely, but our arguments that war was justified in this case were not convincing to them. I was bothered personally, as I have a fundamental dislike for any kind of physical violence. The days leading up to January 15 and until the hostilities ended on February 27 were troubling days for me. I carried out my instructions but had a few sleepless nights.

Once the hostilities ceased, the focus of my discussions with the Holy See were on the postwar situation. And what a wonderful change for Margaret and me! We attended evening Mass on February 27 and thanked God that the hostilities were over. U.S. casualties had been very few. We were uneasy, however, about the rumors that thousands of Iraqis had been killed. But we could now talk about peace.

I told Vatican officials soon after my arrival in 1989 that the Bush Administration had as a foreign policy goal the resolution of the Middle East conflict. I could see that while they did not question our intentions, Vatican officials wondered if the process to resolve the Middle East conflict would ever start. That conflict was rooted in a history of alienation. There were not many optimists who could see a peaceful solution.

The subsequent announcement in September 1991 that the United States and the then Soviet Union would cosponsor a meeting in Madrid in October had a very positive effect on their estimation of our intentions. As soon as the news about the conference broke, both Cardinal Sodano and Archbishop Tauran told me how much the Holy See supported this initiative.

On October 29, I was called to the Secretariat of State by Archbishop Tauran, who gave me a personal message from the Pope to transmit to President Bush. The message was strong. The Pope said:

> I wish to convey to you, as cochairman of the conference which is to begin tomorrow in Madrid my fervent best wishes that the conference will be a real path towards peace ... your efforts and those of your assistants, in particular Secretary of State James Baker, have led to this first important stage, the special significance of which is that it demonstrates a readiness to face in dialogue the grave problems which have burdened the Middle East for decades.

It was very clear that several senior Vatican officials were surprised the conference took place and that the discussions continued between Israel and its Arab neighbors. As soon as the negotiations started, Vatican officials were generous in their praise of the role of the United States in this matter. They were extra-generous in their praise of Jim Baker. This pleased me, as I knew he played a central role in organizing the meeting.

President Bush Visits the Pope

Papal appreciation for the role of the United States in the Middle East discussions was evident in a meeting of President Bush with the Pope on November 8, 1991. The meeting took on a special importance because leftist newspapers and journals, including several Catholic ones, constantly referred to the "coldness" that had developed between the Holy See and President Bush because of their different positions on the use of military force in the Gulf War.

Ambassadors serve as the representatives of their governments. They are also the personal representatives of their chiefs of state to the chief of state of the country where they are accredited. There is the professional desire of an Ambassador to be successful in carrying out his or her mission and instructions.

Needless to say, a visit of the chief of state is always an important assignment for an ambassador. But for me this was especially important.

I knew that the Pope and his senior advisors respected President Bush as a person. They recognized his sound moral qualities as a man, husband, and father. They felt that he was a reasonable, decent, and courageous man. During the first year of my tenure, I made a point when appropriate to communicate these characteristics of George Bush to the Pope and to senior members of his staff.

My connections with the Bush family went back to my student days at The Catholic University of America in Washington, D.C., where the President's father, Prescott S. Bush, Sr., the U.S. Senator from Connecticut, assisted me in obtaining important documents from the Library of Congress for my dissertation. The President's brother, Prescott, Jr., was a trustee of the University where I was President. He was also a close friend. I knew and respected his mother. Needless to say, I wanted the meeting to be successful!

This meeting was also important from the public-perception point of view. The President met alone with the Pope for over sixty minutes. Only thirty to forty minutes had been scheduled. The President briefed the Holy Father on the recent Madrid conference; his goal for a Middle East settlement; the situation in the ex-Soviet Union; China; religious freedom in Saudi Arabia and Haiti. A good part of the meeting was also devoted to the President's ideas on family, community, and moral values.

While the President was with the Pope in the papal library, Secretary James Baker, John Sununu, General Scowcroft, and I were with Cardinal Sodano and Archbishop Tauran in another room.

The same issues were being reviewed by our group. While we had no idea how the dialogue between the Pope and the President was progressing, we knew that our one-hour meeting was very satisfactory.

When the meetings were completed, we joined the President. The President immediately remarked to me that the meeting with the Pope was "great," and I could tell by his smile that it had been very satisfactory. Since the meeting between the Pope and the President had no other participants, it took several weeks before I learned what the two had discussed. The President told his staff that he was very pleased with the outcome.

The original plan was that we would all say good-bye to the Holy Father. Following that, I was to escort the President and Mrs. Bush and Secretary and Mrs. Baker to a nearby meeting room and present them to a group of Americans working at the Vatican and American Seminarians in Rome: a total of about three-hundred-fifty people.

As I was about to do this, I was told by a papal assistant that the Holy

Father would personally escort the President into the meeting room and guide him around the room to meet the Americans. I knew the implications! By making this unprecedented gesture of escorting the President into the meeting room and presenting him to the Americans, the Pope would clear up the rumors, started by several newspapers and magazines, that there was a "coldness" or hard feelings resulting from the Gulf War.

We were overwhelmed by the way the Pope went out of his way to convey this message. After escorting the President around the room, he then praised the President, who of course responded with words of appreciation. As the public meeting ended with the Pope, the President and Mrs. Bush and Secretary and Mrs. Baker said good-bye. The students from North American College then burst out singing "God Bless America." The President stopped and waved again. I knew by the emotion in his "Thank you" that he was pleased with the meeting.

I believe that one reason why the Pope made the unprecedented gesture of escorting the President and Mrs. Bush into the meeting with the three-hundred-fifty Americans was that he wished in a dramatic way to counteract the vicious images that had been conveyed by several idiosyncratic Catholic publications, especially *Sabato*.

The Pope's personal diplomacy signaled his respect for the President and the United States. There had been divergent positions between the Holy See and the United States on how to free Kuwait from Iraq's occupation. The central reason was the objection by the Holy See of the use of war to free Kuwait. The central issue of the use of force, or whether war is ever "just," is still being debated. There still is not a clear statement from the Holy See on this matter. After the Gulf War, there was Somalia and ex-Yugoslavia. The world needs a guideline on when force can be used to solve world problems. Once the conflict ended, the United States and the Holy See cooperated closely in efforts to resolve the complex Middle East problems.

The United States (the world's only real superpower) and the Holy See (the world's only sovereign moral power) had a disagreement on how to resolve the crisis caused by Saddam Hussein. But there were no hurt feelings as each power appreciated the other's overall commitment to a just and peaceful world order. And there were also the realities for these two great powers. There is much injustice in the world that still needs their attention.

CHAPTER VIII

The State of Israel and the Holy See: Complex Relationships

THE INSTRUCTIONS from Secretary Baker concerning Israel were clear and simple. In a brief declarative sentence, he said in his official letter of instructions to me, "You should also urge the Holy See to recognize the State of Israel." Several months before that, while I was preparing for my confirmation hearings in July 1989, I was told that there might be one or two questions for me. Not knowing what the questions would be, I prepared rather thoroughly for the hearing. At the hearing there was only one important question. Senator Joseph Biden, who presided at the committee hearing for my confirmation, brought up the matter of papal recognition of the State of Israel. He strongly urged me to give priority to influencing the Holy See to establish diplomatic relations with the State of Israel. As other senators in the committee hearing looked on, I had no doubt that he was reflecting the sentiments of the United States Senate.

Consequently I had a double-barreled command: both the Secretary of State, the executive to whom I reported, and the Senate, elected by the American people to represent them, wanted me to focus on obtaining a favorable decision of the Holy See to establish diplomatic relations with the State of Israel. I soon found that the history of the Holy See's relationship with the Holy Land, Israel, and neighboring areas had many complicated nuances to it. This was not an easy assignment.

I concentrated on accomplishing this instruction during my tenure as U.S. Ambassador to the Holy See. I had hoped to accomplish it before my departure. While considerable progress was made, I did not succeed in having diplomatic relations between the Holy See and the State of Israel established while I was ambassador. I was able to play a role in establishing dialogue between the two parties and to see the official process that would lead to diplomatic relations initiated. But I departed Rome without accomplishing this main goal.

History

The current position of the Holy See on Israel is rooted in its historical position on the former Palestine and on Jerusalem. In the years preceding, during, and following World War II, the Holy See had a fear that either Arab or Jewish domination would be harmful to Christian interests in the area.

As early as the 1920s and again in World War II, the Vatican expressed grave reservations about plans for establishing a national home for the Jews in Palestine. Similar reservations were expressed in 1944 for plans to create a Pan-Arab Confederation in the Middle East. Again, it was felt that the plan for the Arab League would put the Christian community in a precarious situation. Concern for the welfare of the Christian communities has always been a primary concern of the Holy See in the Middle East. While small in numbers, the Christian Arabs are descendants of some of the first Christians.

Worldwide events moved quickly, and on May 14, 1948, the Jewish people throughout the world rejoiced with the proclamation of the State of Israel. While the Jewish people thus had their homeland, the Holy See remained concerned about the Christians within the State of Israel and those who were displaced, living in nearby areas.

Concern for the human and civil rights of the Arab community — both Christian and Muslim — also remained a top priority for the Holy See.

Another primary concern of the Holy See is the status of Jerusalem and the holy places of the Christian world within and near the city. The Israeli Parliament, subsequent to the Declaration of Independence in 1948, declared that Jerusalem was the capital of the Jewish State. The United States and most countries that have diplomatic relations with Israel have not recognized this and have kept their embassies in Tel Aviv. While the State of Israel has guaranteed the protection of holy places, the Holy See wanted more than a unilateral decision by an Israeli government that could be revoked.

The original Vatican position calling for an international status for Jerusalem has been modified to a call for guarantees of access to the holy places by the international community.

By the time of my arrival as Ambassador in 1989, the concerns of the Holy See about Israel also included the technical "state of war" that still existed toward all its neighbors but Egypt. This included a serious concern for the rights of Palestinian people in the territories occupied by Israel.

Distinction Between Israel and Jewish Matters

Soon after my arrival in 1989, I perceived a clear distinction between Jewish matters and questions involving the State of Israel.

I had frequent visitors from the American Jewish Committee, the Anti-Defamation League (ADL) and other groups representing the American Jewish people. Such groups were generous in their praise of the Holy See's efforts on behalf of human rights and religious freedom in the world. The Pope's voice was a major ally in the campaign against outbreaks of racism and anti-Semitism in Europe in the early 1990s.

But the public perception frequently voiced to me by Jewish and other visitors was that the lack of diplomatic relations between the Holy See and Israel was rooted in some kind of prejudice against the Jewish people.

I knew that this was not the case, and that the only way to clear up the matter was to accelerate the process of diplomatic exchange between the Holy See and Israel. I consequently worked enthusiastically to carry out my instructions from Washington of urging the Holy See to exchange diplomatic representatives with Israel. Two preliminary steps, in my opinion, were important. One was to focus on resolving some of the key differences between the Holy See and Israel. The other was to emphasize that the central problems were between two governments: the Holy See and the State of Israel.

One of the first things that I did was to inform visitors of all religious backgrounds who were interested in the topic that this was a state matter, not a religious one. Catholic-Jewish relations were, in my opinion, fine. This was a matter of relations between the government of Israel and the government of the Holy See.

Efforts by religious groups to campaign for recognition of Israel by the Holy See were counterproductive. Demonstrations at the Vatican, as well as media charges declaring the non-recognition policy by the Holy See to be anti-Semitic, made the efforts of those who were urging diplomatic relations more difficult.

Religious leaders tended to cloud the real issues, which were not religious. Various bilateral problems needed to be resolved. They included, first of all, the future of peace in the Middle East. I knew that there was little chance that the Holy See would exchange ambassadors while the future of the occupied territories was in doubt. My last months of working on this matter were clouded by the Israeli deportation in 1992 of over four hundred Arabs accused of violating various security laws.

Other matters like church property, guarantees for the holy places, and the ending of a state of war with neighboring countries were also on the agenda and needed to be resolved. With attention to those problems, the matter of boundaries between Israel and her neighbors seemed less important as an impediment than previously.

Impact of Madrid Meeting: Visit of Cardinal O'Connor

There was no real movement for change in diplomatic status on the part of the Holy See until the start of the Middle East conference in Madrid in October 1991. As I discussed in the preceding chapter, the Holy See was pleased — first, with the fact of the conference, and then with the concrete results. Once the Madrid Conference started, I regularly briefed Holy See officials on the results.

Several weeks after the Madrid conference, while President Bush was meeting with the Pope, Secretary James Baker and I were meeting with Cardinal Sodano and Archbishop Tauran. When Secretary Baker brought up the matter of diplomatic relations, Cardinal Sodano acknowledged that the Madrid conference established a "new context" — discussions had started between Israel and her neighbors on resolving the conflicts that had been plaguing the Middle East since World War II. President Bush found in his November 1991 meeting that the Pope was pleased with the progress of the Middle East peace negotiations. The President indicated at that time to the Pope that he hoped that these negotiations would lead to a normalization of Israeli-Holy See diplomatic relations.

In the weeks following the November meeting with Cardinal Sodano, I reported to Washington that I found more optimism in Vatican circles for the possibility of resolving the Vatican-Israeli impasse over the establishment of diplomatic relations.

Cardinal John O'Connor, in his role as president of the Catholic Near East Foundation, visited Egypt, Lebanon, Jordan, and Israel in late December 1991 and early January 1992. I knew about the trip from a year earlier, because the then ambassador of Egypt to the Holy See, Ismael Mubarak, at a luncheon I gave honoring Cardinal O'Connor, invited him to visit Egypt. Plans for the trip eventually grew to four countries. It was a very successful visit, in which the Cardinal met with the Egyptian President Hosni Mubarak, Israeli Prime Minister Yitzhak Shamir, Jordan's King Hussein, and Lebanon's President Hrawi and Prime Minister Karami.

On January 8, 1992 Cardinal O'Connor met with Pope John Paul II and briefed the Pope on the great desire for peace among the people in the four countries he had visited. He recommended that the Holy See take steps toward establishing diplomatic relations with the State of Israel. I knew that this recommendation of Cardinal O'Connor would be carefully considered by the Pope because of the Cardinal's influence at the Vatican.

Following his meeting with the Pope, Cardinal O'Connor was my guest at the residence for a luncheon attended by two top Vatican officials, Archbishop Giovanni Battista Re (General Affairs) and Archbishop Jean-Louis Tauran (Relations with States). Other guests included Avi Pazner, Israeli Ambassador to Italy, and Ambassadors of Egypt and Lebanon to the Holy See. In the case of the three ambassadors, it was the first time they had met and shook hands. It was also the first meeting between Israeli Ambassador Pazner and Archbishop Tauran.

Cardinal O'Connor reported on the impact in this area of the new situation caused by the collapse of the Soviet Union as a superpower and the consequences of the defeat of Iraq by the United States-led coalition. I reported to the Department of State that Cardinal O'Connor said "he found a real desire in Israel to make progress on this issue [peace in that power vacuum]. O'Connor pointed out that the status of Jerusalem, the situation of Palestinians, and the status of Christian communities were issues that would have to be addressed."

I knew that Cardinal O'Connor had urged the Pope to begin the process of normalizing relations with Israel. He proposed that a bilateral commission be appointed to study the matter. This would be an intermediary step that could result in the exchange of diplomatic representatives.

Wanting to take advantage of the impetus created by Cardinal O'Connor's visit with the Pope, I met with Israeli Ambassador Pazner on January 15. Pazner told me that Israel would approach relations with the Holy See as it had with Moscow and Beijing. He said the Israelis thought that there should be relations with the Holy See, and also that diplomatic relations would be at least as useful for the Vatican as for Israel. He told me that demands for an international status for Jerusalem are now mentioned less by the Vatican. Pazner said that Israel recognized the Church's real concern about religious institutions and practices, and that this matter could be discussed between the sides.

I maintained contact with the Israeli ambassador and with Vatican officials involved with the Middle East in the following months. There were on-again, off-again starts to name a joint commission but by the spring of 1992 nothing significant had happened.

My Israeli contacts began to show impatience with the lack of movement. Ambassador Pazner, in an interview in the April 1992 edition of the *Catholic World Report*, publicly expressed the concern of the Israeli government at the slow pace of change in Israeli-Holy See relations when he said:

> Here is a fact. Israel has now existed for forty-three years, yet there are still no diplomatic relations between us and the Vatican. I believe there is an ambivalence in the Vatican's attitude as to Israel. For now, Israel is not being treated as all the other countries in the world, while our country is almost universally recognized by the rest of the world.

Visit to Israel

In the spring of 1992 I strongly felt that the time was opportune to accomplish the assignment given to me by the United States government: to influence the Holy See to establish diplomatic relations with Israel. This new atmosphere favoring change was generated by the post-Gulf War peace activities, but I feared there was a danger that these new opportunities were being missed. I felt that both sides needed to see the "big picture" and to move away from details that were turning into major obstacles. After discussing the matter with my staff, I decided to go to Israel.

I consequently requested and received permission from the U.S. Department of State to visit Israel on a "private visit." My wife and I were able to arrange to be included in an Italian pilgrimage group that left for Israel on April 6, 1992. It was a very good arrangement, as the group's one-week visit focused on the Arab-Christian community.

We visited Nazareth, Galilee, Bethlehem, and Jerusalem. Going there "privately," I was able to avoid the complicated aspects of an official visit. I wanted to see the situation at first hand, meet with Arab-Christian leaders, observe the access to the holy places, and make my own assessments.

My wife and I both had the same initial reaction. We felt that there was a yearning for peace among Arabs and Israelis. This was matched by a hope that the end of the old order of the Cold War in the world could help to end the decades-old conflicts that had brought so much suffering to them.

I met with Michel Sabbah, Latin Patriarch of Jerusalem, and could easily see his concern for all Arab Christians within the borders of Israel, and especially for those in the occupied territories. He regarded the Arab Christians as a lonely minority in a society where they had little or no power.

Patriarch Sabbah is a strong leader of his people and frequently a thorn in the side of the Israeli authorities. My meetings with him and the junior Arab Christian leaders convinced me that the longer the occupation of the West Bank continued, the deeper would be the alienation between the two communities.

I also met with the Holy See representative to Jerusalem, Archbishop Andrea Cordero Lanza di Montezemolo. He was more optimistic than Patriarch Sabbah about the prospects of resolving the key issues concerning the occupied territories. He agreed that the longer the occupation continued, the more profound would be the resentment among the Christian Arabs.

Jerusalem, regarded as the Holy City by the followers of Christ, as well as the followers of Judaism and Islam, would be closed to visitors from the occupied territories from time to time. Each time this occurred, there would be resentment among the Christian and Muslim Arabs who could not enter the Holy City.

Israeli government officials were aware of my presence in Israel. I had visited Israel once previously. They cooperated with my plan to be there as a pilgrim, visiting mostly Arab communities. I did, however, spend one afternoon with Moshe Gilboa of the Israeli Ministry of Foreign Affairs.

Ambassador Gilboa reviewed the Israeli position for me. There was nothing new in what he said. He emphasized the public position of the State of Israel. The Israelis are ready to establish full diplomatic relations with the Holy See. My wife and I both felt that he indicated impatience with the slowness of the Vatican response.

My wife and I then visited Yad Vashem, the Israeli museum that documents the horrors of Hitler's genocide against the Jews. This reminded us of our 1990 visit to Auschwitz. A full understanding of the Israeli position on the Holy land, Jerusalem, and related matters requires an understanding of the impact of the Holocaust on the Jewish people.

Most of the Israeli leaders are survivors of Hitler's genocide against the Jews. The concentration and death camps were frequently in locations not far from Christian churches. The memory of more than six million Jews slaughtered in Christian Europe still haunts Jewish leaders. The grotesque nature of the Nazi genocide against the Jewish people in Europe has left a scar in Jewish-Christian relationships, since the predominant Jewish position is that Christians should have done more to ameliorate the crimes against them. It is consequently understandable that some Jewish leaders, both within and outside Israel, would suspect anti-Semitism, at least subconsciously, in the lack of diplomatic relations between the Holy See and Israel.

My attempts to reason with Catholic Arab leaders on the positive aspects of diplomatic relations between the Jewish state and the Holy See were complicated by the appearance in the *Jerusalem Post* on April 10, 1992, toward the last days of my visit there, of a major article on Israeli-Vatican relations.

Below the headline "A History of Malice," the subhead was "Israel-Vatican Ties Must Be Seen in the Context of the Historical Malice and Hostility of the Church Toward the Jews." The article went on to say that "the unwillingness of the Vatican to establish formal relations with the State established by the Jewish remnants of the Holocaust must be viewed in the context of the historical malice, hostility, and animosity of the Church towards the Jews." As a feature article in the prestigious *Jerusalem Post*, it was naturally called to my attention by all the local Arab and Catholic leaders I was meeting with.

Despite all the apparent obstacles to progress in establishing diplomatic relations, I, in my discussions with Arab Christian leaders and with the Apostolic Delegate to Jerusalem, Archbishop Montezemolo, emphasized that in my opinion it was in the interest of the Holy See to establish diplomatic relations.

The many changes in world affairs by 1992 meant that most states in the world had diplomatic relations with Israel. The number that had not extended diplomatic recognition had diminished to a very few states. The three active leaders opposed to diplomatic exchange with the Jewish State were Muammar al-Qaddafi of Libya, Saddam Hussein of Iraq, and Hafez al-Assad of Syria. This, as I pointed out, was not a very respectable group to have associated in any way with the Holy Father. I repeated the same observation to Holy See officials on various occasions.

The Joint Commission

In June and early July 1992 I was able to report to the Department of State that reliable sources at the Vatican had informed me that talks were underway with Israeli officials on the establishment of a joint commission to study the establishment of full diplomatic ties with Israel. In a sixty-day period, I reported the "ups and downs" of their efforts.

The announcement finally occurred on July 29, 1992. My ambassadorial colleagues from the United Kingdom, Canada, Egypt, Lebanon, Iran, and I were called to the office of Archbishop Tauran and informed that a bilateral commission on Holy See-Israeli relations had been established. The archbishop said that it is "an official structure on the beginning of a road which should lead to the normalization of relations."

In my report to the Department of State, I said that Archbishop Tauran indicated that the bilateral commission would study "the rights of the Catholic community in Israel and the occupied territories" and the "juridical status of the Catholic Church in Israel and the occupied territories." Archbishop Tauran said that the Holy See would be sensitive to the needs of other Christian communities but would not "be the spokesman for them."

Archbishop Tauran pointed out, as I reported to Washington, the official position of the Holy See that there must be an internationally recognized guarantee of access to the sacred places of all the faiths in Jerusalem. This represented a modification from the previous Vatican position that Jerusalem should be a free city not subject to the sovereignty of any one country. He also repeated the often-stated position of the Holy See that the rule of law must exist for all peoples in the area, including the Palestinians.

Archbishop Tauran, who was accompanied by Monsignor Claudio Celli, Undersecretary of Relations with States, and Monsignor Luigi Gatti, was emphatic when he pointed out to the diplomats at the meeting that the "Holy See is taking advantage of the fact that Israel and the Arab countries are talking." He said that Israel and the Holy See had decided to work together to "find solutions to the problems of their bilateral relations."

In response to my question, Archbishop Tauran told me that the Holy See "had not changed its conditions for normalization" but that "the international framework had changed." He stressed the importance of the ongoing Middle East peace discussions. He repeated to me what he had previously said: Beginning with the Madrid conference, there was a "new context."

In a personal note attached to my report to the Department of State, I said, "Encouraging the Holy See to establish full diplomatic relations with Israel was one of the assignments given to me. The structure to do this has been established. In the case of Poland, it took four years for a bilateral commission to mature into the exchange of ambassadors. It will not, in my opinion, take so long in this instance."

Fall 1992: Visit of Foreign Minister Peres: Conflicting Evaluations

The movement toward the exchange of diplomatic representatives received an impetus from the meeting on October 23, 1992 of Israeli Foreign Minister Shimon Peres with Pope John Paul II. Israeli Ambassador Pazner told me that the forty-five-minute meeting was "warm and friendly." He described the Pope as "deeply moved" by Peres's invitation to visit Israel. The Pope said that it had been his long-held desire to visit the Holy Places.

In the fall months of 1992, I reported to the Department of State that there was a qualitative difference in the reports our embassy was receiving. It seemed to us that the Israeli evaluations coming from their embassy in Rome indicated a hope to sweep the Vatican toward full diplomatic relations by publicly creating a sense of inevitability. The Vatican, on the other hand, first wanted a number of issues settled to their satisfaction, including guarantees on the church's institutional rights and the status of Jerusalem.

During the fall 1992 months, there were several meetings of subcommittees of the joint commission, working on specific technical problems. Following the November meeting, it was evident from both sides that very little progress was being made.

On November 17, before departing for Israel, Undersecretary Claudio Celli said that the Vatican side was not optimistic but would continue to work on the need to resolve concrete problems as a basis for moving toward full diplomatic relations. He said that one of the reasons for continuing the talks now was to send a positive signal at a time of rising anti-Semitism in Europe.

Israeli Ambassador to Italy Avi Pazner and I were in regular contact during this period. I wanted very much, in the last months of my assignment as U.S. Ambassador to the Holy See, to do everything possible to push forward the process whereby the State of Israel and the Holy See would at long last establish diplomatic relations. Pazner was an activist ambassador and was concerned about the slow pace of the bilateral discussions. The strong official Israeli position was that all the bilateral legal issues could be worked out after the Declaration of Principles was signed and diplomatic representatives exchanged.

Letter of President Bush

Recognizing that we were at a stalemate on progress on Holy See-Israeli relations, I called a meeting of our embassy team in mid-December. Cameron Hume, Deputy Chief of Mission, Damian Leader, Political Officer, Ted Osius III, Administrative-Political Officer, and I spent a full afternoon reviewing plans for our next step: our various options to move progress forward. My staff recommended that I send a direct personal appeal to President Bush. He would be leaving office on January 20, 1993, and he was highly regarded by the Vatican for initiating the Middle East peace process. I knew for a fact that the President fully supported the instructions I had received, that is, to influence the Holy See to establish diplomatic relations with the State of Israel.

We drafted a letter in which the central point was a direct appeal by President Bush to the Holy Father urging him to establish diplomatic relations with the State of Israel. There was a quick response. Within a few days I received the letter, dated December 28, 1992. I was instructed to have it delivered as soon as possible to the Holy Father. The letter was very much along the lines that we had proposed. The President said:

> I applaud your decision to create a bilateral commission with the State of Israel and to work toward establishing diplomatic relations. I understand the real concerns and responsibilities you have in the Holy Land, but I am also confident that, working together with our friends in Israel, you will find equitable solutions to those concerns.

The letter went on to state:

> At this holy season when people of many faiths turn their eyes toward Bethlehem, I encourage you to move ahead toward

establishment of diplomatic relations with Israel. I believe that such a courageous and generous reaction would be appreciated by the friends of peace around the world and would make a significant contribution to the historic process now begun of building peace and reconciliation in the Middle East.

We knew that since the letter was from the President, it would be given immediately to the Pope. We heard that we would have an answer soon. The papal letter was prepared on December 31, but because of the holidays it was not given to me until January 2 when I met with Archbishop Tauran.

The letter was a disappointment to my staff and me and also to the White House. We were hoping for more, but we received only a cautious response to a direct appeal from the President. After exchanging greetings with the President, the Pope said in his letter that the commission was studying the problems of mutual interest and that the normalization should lead to the establishment of diplomatic relations.

Obviously my staff and I were overenthusiastic about what a letter from George Bush would bring in response from the Holy Father. However, we soon learned not to be overly disappointed because, while the letter was cautious and restrained, things soon began to happen that led us to believe that the Holy See was moving in the direction of establishing diplomatic relations with the State of Israel.

I met with Israeli Ambassador Pazner on January 26. He was still committed to doing everything possible to assist the bilateral commission so that the end result would be the establishment of diplomatic relations. The day following my meeting with Ambassador Pazner, I received a phone call from Archbishop Montezemolo, who told me that he had been called by the Holy See to return to Rome for a direct discussion on the progress of the commission and other developments in the State of Israel. The Archbishop was rather positive about the results of the bilateral commission. He said to me, "It is working." He admitted that there were still some tough issues to work out and pointed out that Israel wanted relations quickly while the Vatican first wanted normalization. In my conversation with the Archbishop, I raised the issue of the negative public perception that would become worse if there was a prolonged absence of any progress on the diplomatic front. I pointed out to him that the Holy See was quick to recognize the new governments of Croatia and Slovenia.

I admitted that these two countries offered a different situation from Israel, but I pointed out to him that I was discussing the public perception. I also pointed out to him, as I had with other Vatican officials, that the public perception is that the leaders opposed most vehemently to diplomatic relations with Israel were the heads of Iraq, Libya, and Syria, and that this was not good company to associate in the public mind with Pope John Paul II in 1993.

When I left Rome in March of 1993, I looked at the list of assignments given to me. The assignment of influencing the Holy See to establish diplomatic relations with the State of Israel had only partially been accomplished. I did not realize when I started working on this project that there was a long history of complex relationships involving people, philosophies, religions, and hundreds of years of history. There also were high emotions and some prejudice on both sides. It was my feeling from the very beginning that the Holy See, which I loved and respected, had been ill-advised not to have moved sooner to eliminate the peculiar circumstance of not having diplomatic relations with Israel. The Holy See was one of the few international personalities in the world community that did not have diplomatic relations with the State of Israel.

Several months after I returned to the U.S. in April 1993, a senior Vatican official confided to me that there would be a solution to the lack of diplomatic relations by the end of the year. In October 1993, when I inquired again, he confirmed that there would be an announcement by the end of 1993. This time I learned that Holy See officials were still concerned about the reappearance of anti-Semitism in various parts of Europe. Formal diplomatic recognition of Israel could enhance the role of the Vatican in fighting new outbreaks of anti-Semitism. The informant said it was being done in the "Roman Way," as it was important that there not be the appearance of caving in to outside pressure. I understood the Holy See's sensitivity to external pressures. I had frequently advised Washington of it and found authorities in both the White House and the Department of State appreciative of this concern.

In mid-December, while my wife and I were in Lithuania, we learned that the goal I had worked for during my assignment in Rome would be realized by the end of the year. On December 30 a phone call informed us that the Holy See and Israel had established diplomatic links. We thanked God and celebrated with Lithuanian champagne.

CHAPTER IX

The Nightmare in Ex-Yugoslavia

WHEN CARDINAL Sodano's office phoned the Embassy and said that the Cardinal wanted to see me on October 4, 1991, my staff knew that the lead item on his agenda would be Yugoslavia. Upon my arrival, the Cardinal immediately began with the subject of the tragedy in Yugoslavia.

He noted that on the previous day Croatian President Tudjman had met with the Pope. Sodano told me that the Pope had asked him to speak directly with me about the United States' position on Yugoslavia. The Pope wanted the United States to take a more active role in solving the growing problems of ex-Yugoslavia. Sodano also informed me that the Pope had decided that the people of Slovenia and Croatia had the right to independence, and therefore the Vatican was approaching numerous countries urging them to recognize the independence of these two states.

The Pope's request was at variance with the U.S. position that had started evolving in 1989 when I first arrived at my post. By 1992-93 our positions basically converged. What the Holy See had openly predicted in 1990 occurred, and what the United States wanted in 1990 did not happen. As the ethnic nightmare grew worse toward the end of my tour of duty in Rome in early 1993, our positions became closer.

U.S.A. — Pro-Yugoslavia in 1989-90

As I had read the instructions, briefings, and actions coming from Washington in 1989 and in early 1990, it was clear that the goal of the United States was to keep Yugoslavia together. This coincided with a similar goal of the then Soviet Union.

The American goal was based on a belief, first of all, in the melting pot. In spite of recent history to the contrary, Washington policy makers felt that Orthodox Serbs, predominantly Catholic Croats and Slovenes, Muslims, and Albanians could all live together in one nation state. This ideal was rooted in years of the American commitment to spreading American-type democracy throughout the world. President Wilson, following World War I, was a leading figure in promoting, first of all, the breakup of the Austrian-Hungarian Empire, and then the creation of Yugoslavia.

The 1990 Soviet leaders, on the other hand, saw the Serb-dominated Yugoslavia as their ally and wanted Yugoslavia preserved because it meant a Serb-dominated Yugoslavia. The Soviet leadership had seen in 1990 what American policy ignored: Serbian control of the government structure of Yugoslavia.

I was surprised by the strong advocacy of the Department of State to preserve Yugoslavia, because it was common knowledge that other agencies were predicting the collapse of Yugoslavia. Leading academic specialists believed that Yugoslavia was an artificial creation that, with the end of the communist dictatorship, would fall apart. I wondered why one agency would predict the collapse of a country while another branch of government would advocate its preservation. Leading scholars saw little hope for Yugoslavia as a state. On December 15-16, 1989, at the meeting in Brussels of U.S. Ambassadors stationed in Europe, the Yugoslav matter had been reviewed. The bottom line of the advice given was to preserve the country in some form — at least a loose federation, but one that would preserve the single sovereign state. This again, of course, meant the preservation of the Serb power structure.

This also meant preserving, and in 1989-90 strengthening, the hand of Slobodan Milosevic, the Serbian leader who spoke English well and who had many friends in the U.S. government. Only three years later, in *The New York Times*, Michael T. Kaufman was to describe him as a "war criminal and mass murderer."

Secretary James Baker did not attend the 1989 meeting, but the message of Deputy Secretary Lawrence Eagleburger was candid and clear: Preserve Yugoslavia or it will fall apart and become a model for disintegration in the Soviet Union. The United States consequently in 1989 forecast a disaster if independence were given to the various republics within Yugoslavia. But others in government agencies and academic institutions predicted that the breakup would occur in any case. I, not an expert on the Balkans, asked myself why, if the breakup was inevitable, we did not proceed to assist in seizing the initiative and have the dissolution of Yugoslavia occur without massive bloodshed. On the other hand, the Vatican predicted a bloodbath if immediate steps were not taken to recognize that the end had come to Yugoslavia as it had been known. The United States and the Holy See had distinctly different approaches, but both sides wanted to avoid an ethnic war.

The Holy See's interest was primarily in the predominantly Catholic countries within Yugoslavia — Slovenia and Croatia. This was evident to me, and I felt a natural interest for the Vatican in their coreligionists. The United States and the Holy See agreed on the goal — avoidance of ethnic war in Yugoslavia — but differed on how to achieve this goal.

A Bitter History

Catholics in 1990 comprised approximately thirty-two percent of the population of Yugoslavia but were the overwhelming religious group in Slovenia and Croatia. Serbia was predominantly Orthodox.

During World War II, Croatia had openly collaborated with the Nazis; Croatian nationalists pursued a bloody fight with the Serbian Orthodox. There was a public perception in the West of silent approval by the local Catholic church of the Croatian abuses in World War II, which had included false conversions and hundreds of thousands of deaths.

A similar bleak record of Serbian abuse of Croats had also occurred during World War II, but this was not the general perception in the West. Furthermore, the Serbs were allies in the war against the Nazis.

The then Archbishop of Zagreb, Aloysius Stepinac, had sympathized with the Croatian nationalist regime of World War II. Croat nationalism had always been, in the minds of Serbians, tied to Catholicism. While oppressive Croatian actions in World War II received extensive media coverage, the same was not true for Serbian atrocities. The fact that the Croats had been allied with the Nazis and the Serbs with the Allies was probably the main reason.

Archbishop Stepinac had been arrested after the war and sentenced to sixteen years of forced labor for war crimes. After being released from prison by Marshal Tito in 1951, the Archbishop had gone into voluntary "internal exile" under house arrest rather than leave the country. Shortly after that, Pope Pius XII elevated Stepinac to the rank of Cardinal. Tito, furious with the Pope's action, broke diplomatic relations with the Holy See in 1952.

Relations were reestablished in 1966 after extensive negotiations led on the Vatican side by the then Undersecretary of State Casaroli. The agreement between Yugoslavia and the Holy See included a section in which the Holy See condemned "acts of political terrorism." Tito wanted the church depoliticized in exchange for Vatican freedom to conduct church business without interference. It was a minor grant of religious freedom by Tito. The fact that the Holy See accepted the clause was regretted by local bishops, who regarded it as admitting abuses by the Church during World War II. Senior Vatican officials admitted to me that the behavior of Croats during World War II, especially associating themselves with the Catholic Church, was responsible in large part for the alienation that the Serbian Orthodox felt toward the Catholic Church.

The World War II period of alienation between the Catholic Croats and the Orthodox Serbs left a permanent scar on their relations. Once Tito's iron fist was removed, the breakup of Yugoslavia started, and the old ethnic hatreds quickly reappeared.

Melting Pot

American Government and private leaders in contact with me in the 1989-1990 normally applied the positive American experience of "melting pot" to the dilemma of Yugoslavia. I myself was long active in various interethnic movements, and I responded positively, as I believed in the American experience.

As founder of the Center for Ethnic Studies at Sacred Heart University, I had arranged for courses in the history, culture, and language of various Eastern European countries. Most of the students who took the courses were second-generation Americans and for the most part a mixture of various Eastern European nationalities. Ukrainians, Poles, Lithuanians, Slovaks, Hungarians, Czechs, Croats, and Slovenes had intermarried within one generation in America. Within the American context, the hatreds and fears had melted away.

Vatican Warnings About the Dangers in Yugoslavia

In my first year in Rome I followed my instructions, advocating an effort to keep Yugoslavia together: one state with various nationalities. In the first few months of my assignment in Rome, I frequently asked my Yugoslav and Vatican colleagues what happened to the Christian message when Orthodox Serbs and Catholic Croats would kill each other over ethnic differences. However, in long conversations with senior people involved with the Vatican, I soon came to the conclusion that my instructions might be based on a false premise.

In my discussion of the matter with Cardinal Jozef Tomko, confidant of the Pope, in March 1991, he pointed out how different the situations in both the Soviet Union and Yugoslavia were from the American experience. In the United States, he explained, the melting pot worked for good historical and social reasons linked to America's economic system. The old system of Tito had based its control and belief on the communist party. It had fallen apart, and there was no multinational sentiment in Yugoslavia. I always listened carefully to Cardinal Tomko, as I knew that on these matters he reflected the mind of the Pope. I reported this conversation to Washington.

Two Players

Two diplomats to the Vatican were players in the 1989-1990 period warning me about Serbian ethnic intentions. Soon after my arrival I was contacted by Dr. Stephano Falez, born in present-day Slovenia and married to an Italian, who became a U.S. citizen following his university studies in the United States and then returned to Rome.

Steve, a gentlemen-in-waiting to the Pope, was an intimate of the Vatican establishment. A very successful Roman businessman, he had the flexibility to operate at various levels in the Vatican-Roman power structure. He gave me an extensive analysis of Serbian control (1989-1990)of the Yugoslav government. He also gave me the figures on the overwhelming number of Serbs who constituted the officer corps of the Yugoslav military. I knew that his thoughts and observations reflected the "mind" of the Vatican and so reported to Washington.

Professor Ivica Mastruko was the Ambassador of Yugoslavia to the Holy See when I arrived in 1989. As fellow academics, we soon became good friends, and within months I informed the department that Mastruko saw no future for Serb-dominated Yugoslavia. He was a Croat, and his acceptance of or belief in a unified state was paper-thin. The Ambassador of Yugoslavia lectured me extensively on why the breakup of the state was inevitable.

Break in Papal Policy

By July 1991 the Holy See had shifted its policy to favoring immediate independence. It was evident in 1990 that the Holy See was working to influence other countries to be the first to recognize Slovenia and Croatia. But by mid-1991 the Vatican was taking the unprecedented action of being the leader in the recognition process. Pope John Paul II, speaking at a celebration in the honor of the elevation of twenty-three bishops to the cardinalate, commented on the fighting in Yugoslavia. Speaking about the Croatian and Slovenian peoples, the Pope implied a recognition of their right to independence as the "legitimate aspiration of the people."

The Pope sent Archbishop Tauran to war-ravaged Yugoslavia in August 1991. Shortly after his return on August 13, Tauran told my deputy, Cameron Hume that "Yugoslavia has irreversibly changed form." The Holy See, he said, recognizes the legitimate right of Slovenia and Croatia to decide their future relations with other states. On August 18 the Pope told a group of Croatians at the Vatican that "one more time I assure you, I am close to your legitimate aspirations." The Pope also said that he wished to visit Croatia one day.

I reported to Washington soon afterwards that the Holy See was committed to recognizing the independence of Slovenia and Croatia. U.S. policy, however, remained the same. In response to my reports on the change in Vatican Policy, the Department of State cabled me to inform the Holy See that "the U.S. supports a stable, united, democratic Yugoslavia moving toward a market economy and with full respect for individual human rights." An added caveat was that "U.S. assistance to Yugoslavia will go through the federal authorities." This was the public position of the United States, and consequently my message came as no surprise to Holy See officials.

My reports on Slovenian and Croatian aspirations for freedom and the mockery that the Serbs were making of Yugoslav democracy by their heavy-handed control of the Belgrade government had little impact on the department's decisions in 1990-1991.

Visit of Cardinal Kuharic

Cardinal Franjo Kuharic, Archbishop of Zagreb, was in Rome to see the Pope for several days in December 1991. It was immediately evident that he was there to exert maximum pressure on the Pope to formally and immediately recognize Croatia.

This mounting pressure came at a time when the Holy See was actually inclined to proceed in an unprecedented way. I reported this following a meeting on November 26, 1991, at the Vatican Secretariat of State. Cardinal Sodano had summoned the Ambassadors of the United Kingdom, France, Belgium, Italy, Germany, and Austria to his office. I was also there. He presented us with a memorandum appealing for recognition by our governments of Slovenia and Croatia "within a month."

Cardinal Sodano, accompanied by Archbishop Tauran, forcefully presented the Vatican case. This was the first time in modern history when the Holy See actively campaigned for recognition of new states.

There obviously had been some coordination before the meeting, as German Ambassador Haller, Italian Ambassador Scammacca, and Austrian Ambassador Hohenberg were very supportive of the Vatican position. They indicated that these countries were on the verge of recognizing Slovenia and Croatia.

I listened and asked a few questions. While I felt there was merit in the Vatican approach, I did not indicate this, as I knew the Department of State had serious reservation about the Vatican initiative.

A very unusual aspect of the meeting was the position of Yugoslav Ambassador Ivica Mastruko. He surprised some (but not me, as he had frequently confided this to me) with his characterization of his own government in Belgrade. He referred to the "rump" nature of the current ruling group there. He, the Ambassador, said it was "no longer a government and serving only Serbian military interests."

Ambassador Mastruko went on to tearfully report on the savage killings of Croatians, and he urged all countries to withdraw their Ambassadors from Belgrade as a sign of disapproval. He ended his remarks by saying that the government of Yugoslavia — the government he still represented — was "illegal." In late 1991 Dr. Mastruko renounced his position with Belgrade and became several weeks later the first Ambassador of Croatia to Italy.

When Cardinal Kuharic came to my residence for lunch on December 10, 1991, I knew what the Vatican position was. The Cardinal, an impressive figure, had survived Nazi occupation as a young man in World War II and learned how to endure the harsh communist rule of the early years of Tito.

Cardinal Kuharic had made several visits to the United States and was well-connected with the American hierarchy. He orchestrated a very effective campaign on behalf of Croatian independence, not only among the U.S. Catholic hierarchy but also among the two million Croatian Americans. I heard from both groups, and the message was the same. Croatia had the right to be free and independent. It was always a dilemma for me, as I essentially concurred with the message, but as an

Ambassador I had to be obedient to my government's instructions. The question of recognition of Slovenia and Croatia came up in the conversations of Secretary James Baker with Cardinal Sodano and Archbishop Tauran on November 8, 1991. It was apparent then in the conversations that the Holy See favored early recognition as a means to prevent the situation in Yugoslavia from deteriorating any further. The Secretary was accompanied by General Scowcroft, who obviously did not concur. Concern about Serbian control of the Belgrade government and its "greater Serbia" commitments, as expressed by Sodano and Tauran, had no visible impact on the U.S. representatives at that meeting.

Recognition

The long-expected formal recognition of Croatia and Slovenia by the Holy See occurred on January 13, 1992. There was great rejoicing at this announcement in Rome, as both the ideological right and left and also the center of Roman Catholic circles associated with the Vatican seemed to agree on this issue. I could report no opposition to the Pope's decision within any segment of the international Catholic community.

While the U.S. hierarchy was divided on the U.S. participation in the Gulf War, this was not so on Slovenia and Croatia. In fact, not only the leading members of the U.S. hierarchy but also various Protestant church leaders expressed the same opinion to me. All American church leaders who contacted me in 1990 favored independence for Croatia and Slovenia. The only exceptions were several American Jewish organizations who, concerned about the World War II record of anti-Semitism in Croatia, were reluctant to back its independence.

In the first several months of 1992, following the recognition of Slovenia and Croatia by the Holy See and various European countries, fighting developed in Bosnia-Herzegovina. Here the role of Serbia in sustaining the internal conflict was more manifest. The Pope made more pleas for an end to the fighting. On April 7, 1992, the United States extended official recognition to Slovenia, Croatia, and Bosnia-Herzegovina as independent states. The U.S. indicated it would also recognize Macedonia in the future. Sanctions against these four republics were also lifted.

Macedonia

The very sad situation in ex-Yugoslavia sometimes had its absurd moments. On New Year's Day 1992, Pope John Paul II had his usual message and greetings to the world. One of his words of best wishes for the New Year was given to the people of Macedonia. This small, landlocked country in southern Yugoslavia, like Croatia, Slovenia, and Bosnia-Herzegovina, was campaigning for independence. There was a very negative reaction to the Pope's greeting for the Macedonian people in Greece, with demonstrations protesting papal interference in the internal affairs of Greece.

The Greek Government maintained a tough line, claiming that the name "Macedonia" was inherently Greek property and could not be used as the name of another country.

The Greek Ambassador to the Holy See, Georges Christoyannis, saw me frequently and presented me with books and literature on the subject. Greek Archbishop Iakovos of the United States was in Rome and raised the subject with the Pope. He was later my luncheon guest. The Archbishop was there to give the Pope a message — be careful when it comes to Macedonia. In 1993 there was no papal greeting of New Year's wishes to the people of Macedonia.

While Archbishop Iakovos came to Rome as a spiritual leader of the Greek Orthodox Church in North America, the visit also had some indirect political implications. The Orthodox Church had influence with several governments in the Balkans and the Yeltsin government in Moscow. In several instances, relationships between the Orthodox Church and the Holy See were strained, and this could influence the policies of the governments, especially in Romania and Russia.

Archbishop Iakovos told me that the way bishops had been appointed by the Pope in the former Soviet Union caused apprehension in the Russian Orthodox Church about the Vatican's intentions. I urged him to bring up this matter in his meeting with the Pope.

But the main item for Archbishop Iakavos was Macedonia, as he accepted — in fact, endorsed — the position of the Greek government.

As the situation became more tragic in the Croatian and Bosnia-Herzegovina regions of ex-Yugoslavia, Archbishop Tauran told me that the Holy See considered Serbia as the "unquestioned aggressor" in the fighting. The Serbian Policy of "ethnic cleansing" in Bosnia hit the world like a thunderbolt. It had all the aspects of Hitler's genocide operations against Jewish and other communities.

The U.S. position moved closer to that of the Vatican on Serbian involvement in the fighting in Bosnia. In May 1992 I was instructed to inform Cardinal Sodano that the United States saw the Serbian government as "the driving force behind the polarization of ethnic relations underlying Yugoslavia's ongoing disintegration. We see the current Serbian military use of force as the main obstacle to a genuine cease-fire and a political settlement."

Extensive coverage was given in the media to the U.S. position, as it reflected a significant change. This new U.S. position also made my assignment easier. For almost three years, I had harbored significant reservations about our policy of preserving Yugoslavia. I nonetheless carried out my instructions as the U.S. Ambassador.

This is always an area of great discussion among diplomats — carrying out instructions when you do not agree with them. One school of thought is that an Ambassador should have no policy ideas of his own — only reflect the decisions of his superiors.

I never have accepted this in my diplomatic assignments. It was a challenge for me. While I had ideas of my own, I also very much believed in loyalty to the team. And I was a member of the Bush-Baker diplomatic team.

This new U.S. position was what the Vatican had been saying for some time. Later in May (1992) I was able to inform the Vatican that the U.S. was taking serious steps to pressure Serbia to cease continued aggression against Bosnia.

With the U.N. Security Council admitting Bosnia-Herzegovina, Croatia, and Slovenia to the United Nations in May 1992 and also imposing sanctions against Serbia-Montenegro, there was a coming together of the Holy See, United Nations, and U.S. policies on the Yugoslav problem.

Intervention in Bosnia

On August 6, 1992, Pope John Paul II called for "humanitarian intervention" to "disarm those who would kill." Several days later Cardinal Sodano referred in the Bosnia matter to "rights of humanitarian intervention." He went on to say "the European states and the United Nations have a duty and the right of intervention. This is not to support war but to stop war."

The Holy See's position on the right of the peoples within Yugoslavia to have full sovereignty was constantly repeated by the Pope. On February 3, 1993, on his plane to Benin in Africa, the Holy Father said "there are diverse geopolitical situations, there are diverse dimensions to peoples; certainly each people has this right to self determination, that is, to sovereignty." He said this in referring to the situation in Yugoslavia.

I reported the various papal statements on the merits of intervention in the Bosnia-Herzegovina situation to the Department of State in the last months of the Bush Administration. A senior Vatican official who was pleased with the U.S.-led intervention in Somalia in December 1992, said to me, "Why not Bosnia?" The same official told me in February 1993 that he did not believe the United States would take the leadership in resolving the nightmare of ex-Yugoslavia. I concurred with his observation.

Complicating Aspect of U.S.-Yugoslav History

A very complicating factor for the United States in dealing with the breakup of Yugoslavia in the early 1990s was rooted in the post-World War II relationship. One of the stunning success stories of U.S. foreign policy at the height of the "Cold War" with the Soviet Union was the American success in pulling Yugoslavia out of the communist empire of the Soviet Union.

Yugoslavia remained socialist-left but was independent of Moscow. The United States invested billions of dollars to keep Tito's Yugoslavia out of the Soviet clutches. The American goal was to turn Yugoslavia into a model for the Eastern European countries to follow. None did, but Yugoslavia remained a thorn in the psyche of the Soviets.

I knew that some of the leading career government officials, such as Larry Eagleburger and Brent Scowcroft, had served in Belgrade during this period. When the internal troubles in Yugoslavia started to break out in 1989-1990, the U.S. Ambassador was a highly regarded career diplomat, Warren Zimmerman.

Many other members of the U.S. Department of State establishment had close ties with the Belgrade leadership. During the post-World War II period and after Tito, the power structure of the Yugoslav government was Serb-dominated. This was also true of the officer corps of Yugoslavia. It was overwhelmingly Serbian.

The Department of State was infatuated with the Belgrade leadership. This was a major factor in 1989-1991 that caused the U.S. to hesitate in moving away from the Serb-dominated Yugoslav government. During this time, Slobodan Milosevic, the Serbian leader, consolidated his strength and developed his network of support for the Serbian forces in Bosnia and Herzegovina, who were later to commit such atrocities at Vukovar and numerous other places in both Bosnia-Herzegovina and Croatia.

In many ways, the American position was understandable. There were almost four decades of close working ties between American officials of past administrations, both Democrats and Republicans, and Belgrade.

In late 1990 I was so perplexed by the then U.S. policy that on a return trip to Washington I requested to be briefed again on the various government studies. I had remembered them correctly. One predicted the end of Yugoslavia as a unified sovereign state. Scholarly articles were doing the same. Why, then, was the Department of State still supporting Belgrade? Four decades of close working relationships between Belgrade and Washington resulted in professional friendships that were difficult to break.

Croatian Past

It was not only a matter of infatuation with the Serb-dominated Belgrade government that evolved over almost four decades, but it was the antipathy in the Department of State toward Croatia and the role of Croatia in World War II. I could understand the antipathy because the Croatian leadership of 1940-1945 had allied Croatia with the Nazis. The crimes of Ante Pavelic and his cohorts of the then independent state of Croatia were brutal. Reliable estimates indicate that over a million Jews, Gypsies, and Serbian Orthodox Christians were killed between 1941 and 1945. Croatia was also the home of the infamous death camp known as Jasenovae.

There is still lingering resentment about Franco Tudjman, the current Croatian leader, and his reluctance to condemn the World War II record of Croatia. In February 1994, however, Tudjman apologized for his anti-Holocaust book. The anti-Croatian rationale in the Department of State overlooked one important factor: Only the Serbian leadership in Belgrade had a blueprint for expansion beyond their boundaries, which included the doctrine of ethnic cleansing. "Greater Serbia" thinking, furthermore, had been part of Serbian culture for centuries.

Years 1990-91

As the breakup of Yugoslavia became more evident in 1990 and Serbian expansionism more apparent, the Holy See called for the recognition of the right of the peoples of Slovenia, Croatia, and Bosnia-Herzegovina to their own independent governments. By giving international recognition to these states, the Holy See felt that the international community could exercise greater pressure on these new states to conduct themselves along standards appropriate for European states and not to engage in de facto war.

My Catholicism: a Handicap?

In November 1991, around the time when I was preparing for the visit of President Bush with the Pope, for the first (and only) time during my assignment as Ambassador, I felt that my Catholicism was a handicap in the Yugoslav situation.

An important aspect of my duties as U.S. Ambassador to the Holy See was to pass on the information given to me by Vatican officials. And this was to include my recommendations.

I thought that there was great merit to the Vatican position advocating early recognition of Slovenia, Croatia, and Bosnia-Herzegovina. These countries had their own traditions, culture, and languages. They wanted to be independent. The United States was an ardent supporter of independence for the countries of Africa, Asia, and the Caribbean. If Togo, Benin, and Burundi could be independent, why not the more viable countries of ex-Yugoslavia?

Since the Holy See took a very strong position, especially on the right of predominantly Catholic Slovenia and Croatia to independence, the issue gave the appearance of being a Catholic project. European newspapers reported extensively that the Catholic-oriented governments were supporting the Holy See but that the socialist governments of Europe opposed recognition and supported the U.S. position.

Furthermore, the U.S. hierarchy was totally in favor of the Vatican's position on Slovenia and Croatia. While the U.S. Catholic leadership was divided on the Vatican position on the Gulf War and, years earlier, on the Vatican position on Nicaragua, they were solidly behind the Vatican's support for early recognition of the independence of the republics that made up Yugoslavia.

Since I was known as an active Catholic layperson, I felt handicapped about strongly advocating my own position: that there was merit to the Vatican position and that it was in the best interests of all concerned for the U.S. to recognize the states of the old Yugoslavia as independent and sovereign. I felt that the U.S. should also recognize the duplicity of the Serb-controlled Yugoslav Government.

During my consultation visit to Washington in 1991, I consulted with a longtime friend who was a senior official in the Department of State. He cautioned me against raising policy questions on this matter, as I was already known as an active Catholic and the Department of State leadership group could accuse me of being influenced by my Catholicism and thus representing the Holy See to Washington rather than representing the United States to the Holy See.

He felt that the Pro-Belgrade atmosphere was so strong that I would lose credibility. He was convinced that I would be regarded as a "client" of papal thought and thus my ability to influence policy on all matters would be greatly reduced. This presented me with a tough personal challenge. But within several months, the U.S. policy on ex-Yugoslavia significantly changed. Furthermore, the involvement of the Serbian leaders of the military in terrorist attacks of civilians in Bosnia-Herzegovina was finally recognized by Washington, which announced that it would seek a war-crimes trial for the perpetrators of these atrocities.

The U.S. policy of the 1989-1992 period toward Yugoslavia was motivated by the good intention of preserving the federation. We thought it was in the interests of the people there — especially economically — but the unvarnished fact is that the people wanted freedom in Slovenia, Croatia, and Bosnia-Herzegovina. The plans of outside forces could not be imposed on the various ethnic communities of the old Yugoslavia. After more than four decades of harsh communist-style rule, they, seeing the spread of freedom and independence in the world, were not about to renounce their right to independence. The 1992 U.S. policy change was belated. U.S. policy now more closely parallels the Vatican's policy. The differences are over how to end the nightmare.

Slovenia

Before departing Rome, my wife and I wanted to visit at least one of the new sovereign states of ex-Yugoslavia. We received permission from the U.S. Department of State and spent four days in Slovenia in late November 1992. It was something of a challenge, being in Slovenia even unofficially at a time when you had the title of U.S. Ambassador.

The moment my identity became known, the Slovenes would tell me how much they appreciated the support that the Holy See gave to their aspirations for independence. The follow-up question would generally be: "Why was the U.S. reluctant to recognize us?"

One Slovenian student said that he read about U.S. history and our great respect for freedom and independence. "Why," he asked, "was the U.S. against independence for Slovenia?"

It was difficult to answer these types of questions, but fortunately there is a great residue of affection for the U.S. in Slovenia. I understand the same is true in Croatia. Their resentment against the United States will fade away soon.

But the nightmare in Bosnia grows worse. It is unfortunate that the U.S. and the Holy See differed on how to resolve the Yugoslav difficulties in the early days of the breakup in 1989-1991. But the cooperation that now exists, not only between the Holy See and the U.S. but including the United Nations and the countries of Europe, could lead to the ending of a most obscene situation in the heart of Europe. But at the writing of this book, the hour is late and untold thousands have been killed in a tragic conflict that should have been resolved in the early stages.

As the killings in Bosnia grew to include young children playing in the snows in January 1994, Pope John Paul II on January 23 (1994) called for the world community to consider the use of force to bring an end to the almost daily atrocities occurring there — as, in centuries past, the Pope's predecessors had justified the use of force when a clear, overriding moral purpose was served and when there seemed to be no other way to resolve the problem.

This unfortunate tragedy could present the occasion to reapply the just-use-of-force principle in the modern context.

The December 1993 meeting of NATO in Brussels gave no assurance that the North Atlantic community of states is prepared to intervene for the moral purpose of stopping the bloodbath. When will this obscenity end?

CHAPTER X

Eastern Europe and the Future Role of the Free-Market Economy

WE KNEW that on May 1, 1991, Pope John Paul II would issue his long-awaited encyclical on the decline and fall of communism in Eastern Europe and the future role of the free-market economy. Starting around April 1, Rome was flooded with rumors about the encyclical. Some authoritative leaders of the Catholic community said that it would be a negative attack on the American free enterprise system. In the beginning I ignored the rumors, but by mid-April they were growing to a high fever-pitch level.

A group of American Catholic Clergy who visited me in March thought that the encyclical would be a "blast" against the American free-market system. It was obvious from their comments to me that they wished this would happen. One of the visitors was very critical of Dr. Michael Novak and said the forthcoming document would be very negative about the American free-market system and "put Novak" and the American free-market advocates "in their place." This turned out later to be ironic because in June, when Dr. Novak was in Rome after the issuing of the encyclical, I was contacted by the Pope's private secretary to find him, as the Pope wanted to see him and to express his appreciation to him for his articles and books on culture, freedom, and the economy.

The situation came to a boil the last week of April when one of the American wire services carried the story that the forthcoming encyclical would criticize the American private-enterprise system and other aspects of the American socioeconomic way of doing things. Needless to say, I began to receive inquiries from private groups and citizens in the U.S. and in Europe.

Although I received no official request either from the Department of State or the White House on the forthcoming encyclical, I decided that it was in the interest of United States to find out exactly what the document would say. Fortunately, I knew the person who played a major role in drafting the encyclical, and after contacting him I was able to obtain a copy of the final draft. After reading it, I was able to inform the White

House and The Department of State that I thought the United States government would be pleased with the document, and that there certainly would be no "blast" against the American system.

I knew the ideas and philosophy both of the current Holy Father and the evolution of Church teaching, starting one hundred years ago with Pope Leo XIII in *Rerum Novarum*, followed forty years later by Pius XI in *Quadragesimo Anno*, and continued by John XXIII in 1961 in *Mater et Magistra* and by Paul VI in 1967 in *Populorum Progressio*. The 1991 encyclical, *Centesimus Annus*, was a continuation of one hundred years of papal thinking. Since I believe strongly that none of the journalists who were circulating the reports about a very negative document, as far as the United States was concerned, had any access to the early drafts of the encyclical, it is difficult for me to give any rational reason for the very inaccurate prediction of what the encyclical would say. The report of a wire service was so erroneous in its analysis — that the encyclical would be highly critical of the contemporary economic policies as practiced in the United States — that I wondered if there was a deliberate effort to sabotage the document before it was released. Of course I had no evidence of any such plot, but I am still suspicious of the fact that without any real knowledge of the encyclical a leading wire service and several columnists were predicting that it would be a major attack on the United States economic system as personified in the Reagan and Bush Administrations.

Fortunately these reports were not picked up by most of the wire services in the U.S.A. However, the one wire-service story came to the attention of American reporters in Rome, and they were in contact with my staff and with me. By April 27, I felt that I had to take immediate action to prevent a major public-relations mishap.

By happy coincidence, we were having a reception at the residence. I added the names of a dozen or so press members accredited to the Holy See and invited them (even though Margaret wanted me to avoid having large receptions for a few months so we could conserve our entertainment funds for a reception on July 4).

In my previous position as a university president, we had learned how we could entertain with dignity at a cost within our always modest budget. We purchased a large amount of American champagne (a very unknown brand name) and had the waiters serve it with cool towels wrapped around the bottles.

Normally our guests thought that we were serving the best champagne in high-fashion style. If someone should ask to see the label, the waiter would remark that it was a rare (and by implication, expensive) American brand.

My last-minute decision to have the reception was worth the effort. I knew the press representatives and focused on them. I quoted by memory from the advance copy of the document. I learned later that none of the inaccurate, negative reports on what the encyclical would say came from Rome.

And on May 1, *Centesimus Annus* was released and was well received throughout the world. Pope John Paul II strongly condemned communism, pointed out the serious weaknesses of classical nineteenth-century capitalism and praised the contemporary free-market system. There was high praise for it in the Eastern European and ex-Soviet Union countries as giving an accurate analysis of the failure of the communist system.

Comment on the Fall of Communism in Central and Eastern Europe

Referring primarily to Central and Eastern Europe, the Pope reviewed the major factors in the fall of these oppressive regimes:

1. The economic system was inefficient — a consequence of the violation of human rights related to private initiative, to ownership of property, and to freedom in the economic sector.
2. The causes were more than economic. They were linked also to cultural and natural rights and, above all, to the spiritual void created by atheistic communism. This has been a constant theme in the Pope's speeches on this subject.
3. The fall of these regimes was won by peaceful means, a triumph of truth and justice that would have been impossible without trust in God.

The belief that the old communist-bloc countries were inherently weak and ready for collapse had been the central item of conversation between President Reagan and Pope John Paul II in their meeting on June 7, 1982. The American President and the Pope were united in their commitment to free all of Eastern Europe from communist domination. They had different roles to accomplish this goal. The end for communism in Eastern Europe occurred after Reagan left office in 1988, but at the

Vatican I always found an appreciation for President Reagan's role.

1989: Worldwide Importance

The reasons for the weakness of communist control in Eastern Europe were many. Pope John Paul II emphasized how the workers' movement in these countries had fallen under the dominance of Marxism. He felt that the natural consciousness of the workers, energized by the teachings of the Church, had emerged into a demand for justice and dignity. Going back to his early years in Poland, Pope John Paul II always believed that Catholic social teachings would touch the conscious of the workers in the communist-dominated countries, and that when the opportunity came, they would throw off the communist yoke. Pope John Paul had a horror of the use of war to change unjust political situations. He was a personal witness to the brutality of the Nazi war against Poland. He was deeply committed to bringing freedom to his homeland through strategic political tactics, but he never advocated, even in the most difficult periods of the communist control of Poland, the use of war to change the system. I saw clearly in the Gulf War the deep feelings that he had about using war to resolve international disputes.

I remember in my first meeting with the Pope in October 1989 that he had then seen clearly the communist house of cards falling apart. He commented to me that it was strange that some countries in Latin America were still following the Marxist ideology. But he said with a smile that things would change there also. I told my wife, following this first meeting with the Pope, that he was quietly confident in what he said and predicted! This remained true throughout my time in Rome.

The Pope recognized that there was a sincere desire on the part of some for a compromise between Marxism and Christianity, but this, he said, was impossible. While extensive dialogue had been carried out with the Eastern communist countries in the 1960s through the late 1980s, there was never any compromise by the Holy See on fundamental principles. Cardinal Casaroli, who was the major intermediary between the Holy See and communist regimes during that period, told me that while Holy See officials were courteous and saw points of convergence in the conversations, there never was any compromise on basic principles and policies. In the 1970s and the 1980s when Cardinal Casaroli and other Vatican envoys would meet and dialogue with the then communist leaders of the Soviet Union and Eastern European countries, they would be polite and courteous. Some within the Church thought they were compromising. But they did not compromise on any essential principle. They knew how to say no with a nice smile. Politeness does not mean surrender on important principles, and that had been true in this situation.

This loyalty to principle was reflected in the strong position that the Pope took against liberation theology in Latin America. Again, in my October 1989 meeting with the Pope, he had referred to the several countries in Latin America that still practiced Marxist ideology as victims of the failed communist economic system. He simply said that they would soon begin the process of change as the Eastern Europeans were doing.

The encyclical contained a clear warning by the Pope that there was a danger that social, regional, and national conflicts would erupt in the wake of the collapse of the old communist dictatorships. He called for assistance to the Central and Eastern European countries, as their crippled economies were not their fault but the consequence of tragic historical circumstances. The United States, Germany, and other countries initiated various assistance programs at the end of the 1980s for the countries that overthrew their communist dictators. The tragedy of the fighting that occurred after the break up of Yugoslavia was one that was implied in papal statements made around the time this encyclical was issued.

But the Pope was strong in cautioning that the efforts to help Eastern Europe should not distract from aid to the Third World. In the 1990s Pope John Paul II's voice on the needs of the African people for assistance was constant. He mentioned it to me in my first meeting with him in 1989 and in my last meeting with him in 1993. The disarming of the huge military machine of the East-West conflict, in the Pope's view, would make enormous resources available for this kind of assistance. In actuality, the internal needs of United States, Great Britain, France, and Canada for transition to the post-Cold War era consumed much of the peace dividend. No major funds were thus available from the major industrial countries for the rebuilding of the Russian and Eastern European economies.

The worldwide recession that hit the United States in 1991 and then expanded to Europe in 1992 and 1993 was very evident to the Vatican. I think this was the main reason why in the periods following the encyclical I never received any pressure from Vatican officials to push the point of view that the United States and Western European countries should significantly increase their economic assistance to the Eastern European countries and the new countries of the old Soviet Union. Despite the lack of pressure, I did keep the Vatican informed about assistance programs launched by the U.S. government in Eastern Europe, like the extension of the Peace Corps or programs to encourage investment flow, and also the programs of private organizations assisting the Eastern European countries.

Within weeks of my arrival in Rome in 1989, I became a close observer of the sweep of freedom in Eastern Europe. I personally regretted that there did not seem to be the national will to mount a massive economic assistance program such as the U.S. launched in Europe following World War II. And the Western Europeans did not have the will either. Personally and confidentially, I shared these views with Vatican leaders.

Role of Free-Market Economy

The more important part in this encyclical was the Pope's discussion of private property, capitalism, and the free-market economy. Various American groups with their own agendas were in Rome in 1989-90 attempting to influence the Pope and his staff on what he should say about the free-market economy. It was known that there would be a document in 1991. While he consulted with advisors and one Italian intellectual who was very influential, the conclusions in the encyclical sprang from his own Catholic social-justice principles. Once the document was made public in 1991, the same groups tried to influence interpretations that supported their own points of view. The Holy See was able to steer clear of the special-interest groups and I was able to avoid being used by the same groups. I represented the United States government and had no instructions to influence papal preparation for the encyclical. I also had no instructions to influence the interpretations. I was, however, approached by one private U.S. organization. The representative said to me, "You are trusted by the Vatican, and you ought to do this!" I looked at him rather coldly and quietly pointed out that I represented the U.S. government and not private interest groups.

When the various rumors started circulating in April 1991, I felt that I should find out what it would say and so report to Washington. I did that two days before the encyclical was issued. I was frankly amazed at the pushing and pulling of Catholic groups trying to influence the final edition of the encyclical. I was equally pleased to witness the ability of the Vatican to withstand such pressure.

The Legitimate Role of Property and Profit

In discussing private property, *Centesimus Annus* calls attention to a new form of ownership — the possession of know-how, technology, and skills. The wealth of the industrialized nations is based more and more on this type of ownership rather than natural resources.

The Church acknowledges the legitimate role of profit as an indication that a business is functioning well. But that, for the Pope, is not the only criterion. Other human and moral factors must be considered. This was not new doctrine, as it is a fundamental teaching rooted in centuries of Catholic teaching. Pope John Paul II emphatically reaffirmed it in this document.

The encyclical warns that consumer attitudes can be created which damage physical and spiritual health. The dangers of excessive consumerism have been an historic concern of the Church. The growing materialism in Western Europe, the United States, and Japan is a worry for the Holy See. It came up more than a few times in my discussions with Vatican officials.

The encyclical calls for education of consumers, their responsibility to be selective, and thus to lead a more balanced life. The Pope and his predecessors have felt for some time that the total sociopolitical environment of many parts of the world is excessively hedonistic.

This is one of the most difficult themes to discuss with young people. The acquisition of property, a modern car, fashionable apartments, summer and winter vacations are on the "want" list of millions of young adults in the Western world.

I was the president of a university that proclaimed itself as committed to the values of the Catholic Church. But frequently I felt that many of the students had only one interest: the ability to earn an affluent lifestyle.

I spent many hours negotiating for the admission of one of my students to a prominent Ivy League law school. He came to my office to thank me the same day he received his acceptance letter. He told me how delighted he was, because with a law degree from that university he would be able to earn within a few years a "six-figure" income.

This symbolizes the dilemma facing Catholic institutions of higher learning. Despite the emphasis on Judeo-Christian values, so many

Catholic college and university graduates have become addicted to an expensive lifestyle. And many were seduced by hedonism.

The Pope is concerned about the way materialism has so overwhelmed societies where Christianity is supposed to be the foundation of the local culture.

He pointed this out in his analysis of the dangers of capitalism. I was surprised when, within the framework of the praise that he had for the free-market system, a very small but articulate minority resented his criticism of excessive materialism.

This is the role of the Pope. He should be able to offer his opinion on the strong points and failings of all geopolitical and economic systems.

The historical experience of socialist countries has demonstrated, in the analysis of the Pope, that *collectivism* increases alienation. The grave problem of alienation is that it represents a deep rupture in the relationship of people with people — a human condition that papal teachings have always warned about. This is a strong rebuke of the communist system of collectivism.

Alienation also exists in Western societies. In consumerism, people are seduced by their gratification. Alienation is also present when work is organized to ensure maximum profits, with no concern whether the worker grows or diminishes as a person. Exploitation in the forms analyzed by Marx, the Pope believes, has been overcome in Western society. However, alienation still exists when people use one another, or when they seek satisfaction of their individual or secondary needs while ignoring the principle and authentic teachings for being in the world. Permeating the encyclical was an emphasis on community values and the common good rather than focusing only on the individual.

While the Pope has recognized the dangers of consumerism, he implies that it is not an error of the system but rather a weakness of human beings. This is a major difference from his criticism of collectivism, which he condemned because the philosophy is wrong.

The Role of the State and Privatization

Pope John Paul II clearly limited the role of the state. The encyclical declares that the state should provide for defense and preservation of common goals, such as the natural and human environment. There are, in his opinion, collective and qualitative needs that, by their nature, cannot be bought and sold and therefore cannot be safeguarded simply by market forces.

He goes on to state that it is the responsibility of the state to guarantee individual freedom and private property, as well as a stable currency and efficient public services. And in a clear endorsement of the free-market system, the Pope said that while the state should oversee the exercise of human rights in the economic order, primary responsibilities belong to individuals and associations. The state has a duty, in his opinion, to sustain business activities by creating conditions to ensure job opportunities by stimulating these activities where they are lacking or by supporting them in moments of crisis. He would see a proper role for the state to enact measures that create more jobs in an economic recession like the one that afflicted Europe and the U.S. in the early 1990s.

In exceptional circumstances the state can exercise a substitute function in the economic order, but such interventions must be as brief as possible, in order to avoid the tendency to permanently take over functions that properly belong in the private sector. It also should be as brief as possible to avoid enlarging excessively the sphere of state intervention to the detriment of both economic and civil freedoms. There is in the encyclical a strong warning about the danger of the welfare state and the social-assistance state. By intervening directly and depriving society of its responsibility, the social assistance state leads to a loss of human energies and an inordinate increase of public agencies which are dominated more by bureaucratic ways of thinking then by concern for serving their clients, and which are accompanied by an enormous increase in spending. In this regard, there is a clear parallelism between the Pope's evaluation of the weakness of the welfare state and the prevailing majority American political consensus on this matter.

There is frequently a troubling conscience problem for many clerical and lay leaders of the Catholic Church from the United States and Western European countries. I am one of those so troubled. We benefit from the success side of free-market economy. Within three generations many of the grandsons and granddaughters of the late nineteenth-century and early twentieth-century Catholic immigrants have risen to upper-middle-class income brackets. Some now rank among the wealthiest people in the United States.

Catholic social teaching, on the other hand, constantly reminds Catholics about the inequities between the wealthy and the poor. Now, with instant communications and the end of great geographic distance, the poor of the Third World and the wealthy of the industrial states are next-door neighbors.

Americans, furthermore, do not have to look abroad to see the disparity in income. The underclass in the United States, with its below-the-poverty-line existence, is a daily reminder of the great gap in the standard of living that is at the American doorstep. Papal messages have constantly reminded the world that these severe gaps in living standards are not moral and should be corrected.

Vatican officials concerned with the peace and justice issues in their candid talks with me were especially distressed that so many African-Americans remain in the underclass for generations. No one implied that this was a result of a deliberate policy. The same officials were aware of and discussed with me the challenge facing the Catholic Church in the major American cities, where race and poverty seem to be united in a permanent alliance.

Several left-wing lay and clerical Catholics connected with Vatican-related organizations were frankly very disturbed that the Pope did not speak or even hint at the "American scandal" of urban poverty and race in *Centesimus Annus*.

Ten days after the encyclical was issued, a Central American cleric stopped me at a reception and said sarcastically, "Congratulations, you Americans got a whitewash of your unjust system."

He gave me a compliment that I did not deserve and that I would not want. The role of the Pope as an authoritative voice reflecting the historic Christian concern on social justice matters must be free of the manipulations of any state — big or small.

Pope John Paul II was candid in his declaration about the failure of communism. He also cited the deficiencies of twentieth-century capitalism that had no social restraints. He called for an economic system that recognizes the fundamental and positive role of business, the market, private property, and the resulting responsibility for the means of production. This would, for him, provide for free human creativity in the economic sector. The bleak rumors about a papal encyclical that would strongly attack the United States and the free-market system did not occur. In fact, instead we have in the words of Dr. Peter L. Berger, Director of the Institute for the Study of European Culture at Boston University, a "a politically significant text" that leads to the conclusion that what has happened here is a "very important breakthrough in Catholic teaching about the modern world."

This papal document was greeted by the liberal and conservative camps alike as an historic benchmark that forcefully rejected communism and totalitarianism as economic and political models.

As I look back on my experience with the intrigues that surrounded those Americans and others trying either to influence the content of *Centesimus Annus* or attempting to manipulate the interpretations of what the Pope said, I must state my admiration for the papal system that protected the Pope from these intrigues.

Centesimus Annus reflects serious papal reflection on the fall of communism and the future role of the free-market economy. I felt strongly that my role as the U.S. Ambassador was to find out what the document said and to see that it was honestly reported. Despite various attempts to sabotage what the Pope wanted to say, *Centesimus Annus* accurately speaks to the world on the key issues of communism, capitalism, and the free-market economy.

CHAPTER XI

The Holy See and Worldwide Humanitarian Concerns

A S SOON AS the Disabilities Act of 1990 was enacted as legislation by the United States Congress, I looked for ways to involve the Pope and the worldwide Catholic network in ameliorating discrimination against the disabled. I knew that this legislation meant a lot to President Bush. It was a major project for him, and there was excellent bipartisan support for his proposal.

But I also had a personal reason for promoting this cause with the Holy See. My father was born with a partial upper palate and consequently had a major speech impediment all of his life. The word in our working-class neighborhood of Norwich, Connecticut, was that my dad "talked funny." Later in life, as a young adult, I urged my father to consider several medical procedures that could improve his speaking situation. But these attempts essentially failed. He lived his whole life with a disability, and it impacted on him and the whole family. With that memory always fresh in mind, I developed a program for the disabled at Sacred Heart University soon after I became President in 1976. I participated in the conference on the handicapped called by President Carter in 1978. Here I saw the opportunity to blend my personal interest in the disabled with the official policy of the United States government. The interest that President Carter energized in his administration evolved into the law of the country under President Bush in 1990.

I followed the legislative evolution of the Americans With Disabilities Act. I knew that it was a model, not only for the United States but for the industrial world. My goal was to showcase it in an international setting.

I saw a great potential with the annual international conference of the Pontifical Council for Pastoral Assistance to Health Care Workers. Started in 1987, these conferences allowed the Pope to use his moral influence to proclaim what the world community should do. Past conferences had been dedicated to such problems as AIDS and mental health.

My opportunity came in late 1991 to suggest that the problems of disabilities should be the theme of the 1992 conference. I wanted the momentum begun by President Bush in the United States in 1990 to be expanded to the world. Former Attorney General Dick Thornburgh and his wife, Virginia, were our guests at the residence in Rome in November 1991. Ginny had previously told me that their adult son Peter had had a serious accident as a young child resulting in a serious permanent disability. She and Dick had devoted a good part of their lives to empowering their son to lead as normal a life as possible. She was also deeply committed to inspiring society to guarantee all civil rights to members of the disabled community.

Having arranged an audience for Dick and Ginny Thornburgh to see the Pope, I suggested that she bring up the subject of the 1992 conference and recommend a theme to Pope John Paul II. She did exactly that and urged the Pope to dedicate the 1992 conference to the disabled in the world. We followed up on their meeting with the Pope and had a second meeting with Cardinal Fiorenzo Angelini, the head of the Pontifical Council. Mrs. Thornburgh was equally convincing in her meeting with Cardinal Angelini.

I told Ginny Thornburgh, when she and her husband left to return to the United States on November 24, 1991, that I was confident we would have a favorable response. We did. Cardinal Angelini phoned me in January 1992 and told me that the Pope had decided that the theme for the November 1992 conference would be *"The Disabled: All Members of the Body of Christ."*

We at the embassy were delighted because for the second successive year the Holy See was sponsoring an international conference on a topic of real concern to the United States. My first priority had been to influence the Holy See to take a very active position against drug addiction and the international drug trade. We had done this, and the cooperation had been superb. The 1991 Vatican-sponsored Conference on Health Matters had been dedicated to drug and alcohol addictions.

Nine Thousand Disabled to Rome: 1992

It was a very moving experience. They came by plane, train, bus and car — nine thousand participants from ninety-nine countries drawn to the conference on the disabled from November 19 to November 21, 1992. It was difficult to hold back tears seeing the throngs in wheelchairs, the blind with canes or guide dogs, the monitors translating the speeches into sign language.

In addition to welcoming the official U.S. participants — Dr. Louis Sullivan, Secretary of Health and Human Services, Dr. Antonia Novella, Surgeon General of the United States, and Commissioner Deborah McFadden — I went to the airport to welcome Dr. Allan A. Reich, president of the National Organization on Disability, and his wife, leaders of the private U.S. participation in the conference. Americans from all religious faiths were there, including Mary Jane Owen, director of the National Catholic Office for Persons with Disabilities, and The Reverend Harold Wilke, a leading Protestant figure in the movement to assist the disabled.

As we approached the opening session, we could see the anticipation among those who were there: the deaf, the many who could not speak, the blind, the columns of those wheelchairs, the cases of very serious disability. They were attending the first worldwide conference sponsored by an international religious body.

The goal of this conference, like those of its predecessor conferences, was to energize action in countries throughout the world. The strategy included the use of the Pope's moral power with modern communications and with an assortment of prominent people associating with him in proclaiming what should be done.

I distributed copies of the 1990 U.S. legislation, The Americans With Disabilities Act, to the Ambassadors of the industrial countries, as I felt our legislation should be a model for them. The closing address by Pope John Paul II called upon all states and all governments to respect the rights and the personhood of all "our brothers and sisters" who are disabled.

These international conferences, making optimum use of modern communications, were ideal ways for the Holy See to wield its moral influence for goals that the United States and all civilized nations advocated.

Drug Addiction

In the case of the conference on the disabled, I knew that the United States was interested in this subject because of the legislation and President Bush's personal interest. Actually, I had never received any formal instructions from the State Department on this matter but proceeded on my own, knowing that the U.S. government would be interested. Earlier, in the matter of drug addiction, I had received very specific instructions. They were included in a letter to me from Secretary Baker. The instructions had basically urged me to increase the interest of the Holy See in the campaign against drug addiction.

Actually this had not been a difficult assignment, as the Holy See had indicated its concern about the growing alienation in society and the increased use of drugs. Before arriving in Rome in 1989, I had studied the record and read some of the Holy Father's significant statements.

On November 22, 1981, Pope John Paul II had declared that "society today risks being more depersonalized and inhuman and having negative results in many forms of escapism — like, for example, alcoholism and drugs and terrorism." Later, on March 31, 1985, in a letter to young people during the International Year of Youth, he had warned about the "illusory worlds of alcohol and drugs," and again on December 7, 1987, he had warned about becoming "slaves to drugs." In my first meeting with the Pope in October 1989, I raised the problems of drug addiction and drug trafficking. Pope John Paul II spoke forcefully to me about his feelings. I felt by the very tonal quality of his voice that he had a deep personal commitment to ameliorate this grave problem. I knew that the United States had a very strong ally in the battle, and I so informed Washington. All aspects of the drug problem were discussed with various Vatican officials in 1989 and in 1990. The Pope took advantage of many speaking opportunities to work in his concerns about drug addiction and its causes.

Consequently, it was no surprise when the Pope announced in 1990 that the 1991 conference would be dedicated to drug and alcohol addictions. I was personally delighted, of course. I saw this as a clear example of ways the Holy See and the United States could cooperate in the very important field of social justice. Needless to say, both the White House and the Department of State were equally pleased, as President Bush had made the war against drug addiction a major goal in his administration.

Dr. Louis Sullivan, Secretary of Health and Human Services, and Attorney General Dick Thornburgh were among those who participated in this conference.

A Sensitive Matter

One sensitive matter arose in the final days of preparation for the conference. Cardinal Angelini alerted me to the concern of the drug-producing countries. Led by the Bolivian ambassador to the Holy See, they were worried that they would be held as the major culprits, since so much of the basic drug product is produced in Bolivia, Colombia, and Venezuela. I met with this group of ambassadors, and I could see their fear that they would come out of the conference with a very bad image. They felt that for centuries these coca-leaf products had been growing naturally in their countries and that it was only in the past several decades that this growing of coca constituted a problem. The ambassadors frankly told me that they feared that the public perception would be that the producing countries would receive most of the blame for the drug evil in the world. They admitted that it was a grave evil, but they wanted "their side of the story" to be heard. The ambassadors wanted to be sure that consideration would be given to the economic impact of a sudden decline in the production of these coca plants.

I agreed to participate with the South American ambassadors in a round-table discussion on the problem of transferring the agriculture interest of the farmers in these countries to crops that would produce alternative sources of revenue. The United States' role — as a major consumer prepared to pay exorbitant prices for the products that would lead to drug addiction — also came up in discussion. The South American ambassadors naturally wanted "consuming states" like the U.S.A. to share a heavy part of the scandal of the international drug trade.

Once it was known in the Department of State that such a forum would take place and would be available to the worldwide media, there was fear that there would be a outburst of anti-American rhetoric. Despite the misgivings of my colleagues in the Department of State, I was not prohibited from participating in the forum. Once the forum took place, none of the fears materialized. It was a mature discussion of the problems facing these developing societies in finding substitute agricultural production. The standard of living for these farmers was already at the poverty level. I was able to point out the assistance being given by the United States. There was general agreement that the worldwide evil of drug addiction required all countries in all societies to do what they could do to reduce the menace. My preliminary one-on-one contacts with the South American ambassadors seemed to have assured them that the conference would not place the blame on them for the international drug menace.

The Pope focused on the heart of the problem of addiction at the conference. He spoke frankly and with great meaning. There was no doubt in the minds of the U.S. delegation that he saw it as a great contemporary evil. His words were widely acclaimed on November 23, 1991, when he said:

"The alcoholism and drug picture has grown out of all proportion, and today we are faced with insidious social plagues which have spread throughout the world, fostered by vast economic interests and sometimes political ones as well. While many lives are thus consumed, the powerful drug lords arrogantly abandon themselves to luxury and dissipation."

Justice and Peace

The Pontifical Council for Justice and Peace is an agency of a government of the Holy See with which the U.S. Embassy had many contacts during my tenure in Rome. This body reflects the concern of the Church on social questions. The birth of this council is rooted in Vatican II's Pastoral Constitution on the Church in the Modern World, *Gaudium et Spes* (n. 90):

"Given the immensity of the hardships that still afflict a large part of humanity, and in order to foster everywhere the justice and love of Christ for the poor, Vatican Council II suggests that it would be most appropriate to create an organization of the universal Church whose task it would be to arouse the Catholic community to promote the progress of regions of the world that are in need and foster social justice among nations."

The Justice and Peace council reflects on the social teachings of the Church. It is not an operational agency but sets forth Church teachings on contemporary matters and thus is an energizer of the worldwide Catholic network.

The publications of this papal agency include comprehensive texts on foreign debt, homelessness, and racism. Coming from the Holy See, these texts reflect the universal teaching of the Catholic Church.

My contacts with Cardinal Roger Etchegaray, president of the Council, were on the human rights problems in Liberia, Sudan, Ethiopia, Saudi Arabia, Zaire, and South Africa. A former Archbishop of Marseilles, Cardinal Etchegaray is an influential member of the Pope's government. All members of the embassy staff were in frequent contact with his staff while I was the Chief of Mission. I saw the Cardinal frequently.

The Pontifical Council for Justice and Peace serves as a think tank for the Pope. Many of the Pope's statements on poverty, disease, racial matters, or dehumanization find their origin here.

A central theme of the council was that to correct the inequities in the world there must be a redistribution of the world's resources. This concept was a concern to Washington. Both the Democratic and Republican administrations were not totally pleased with the papal emphasis on the redistributions of the earth's resources, as this was interpreted as meaning that countries like the United States would have to do with less so that the countries in the southern hemisphere and other developing societies could have more.

In preparing for my assignment in 1989, I discussed the objection of the Department of State to this emphasis. I was told that I should try to influence the Holy See to reduce its advocacy of redistributing the world's resources and to suggest that the Church give greater emphasis to augmenting the world's resources: suggesting ways for developing societies to follow free-market strategy so that they can increase their living standards without asking the developed and industrial nations in any way to decrease their living standard.

I personally felt that the Department of State position was slightly naïve, as I did not really believe that it would be possible to correct the inequitable distribution of the world's resources without the wealthiest nations making a greater sacrifice. On the other hand, I knew that it would be most difficult politically for the United States government under any administration — Democratic or Republican — to advocate its willingness to give up part of our standard of living so that the peoples of the Third World could have more.

As I said, I was perplexed by the U.S. government's instruction and decided not to raise the matter with Holy See officials. I knew that our position would be incomprehensible to them, as there was nothing new to the papal position. It is rooted in centuries in Church teaching on social justice. The Western countries, despite the fact that their culture is rooted in Judeo-Christian values, find it difficult to ask their citizens to sacrifice any aspect of their standard of living for the peoples in developing societies.

There was no question in my mind that the developing societies need to do more to assist themselves. Free-market strategies have certainly been more successful in Asian countries like Taiwan and Indonesia than socialism was in Tanzania and Zambia. But I also felt that the Western countries and Japan could be doing more to reduce the gap between the rich and the poor in the world.

Again, on August 11, 1993, while visiting Jamaica, the Pope made a strong plea for the redistribution of the world's resources so that there can be a better standard of living. He made these remarks on the eve of his visit to Denver, Colorado, where he would meet U.S. President Clinton for the first time.

Refugees

The Pontifical Commission for the Pastoral Care of Migrants and Itinerant Peoples' is another agency with which the embassy cooperated. Assistance to refugees and immigrants has historically been a great concern of the Vatican. The early centuries in Europe were times when the Holy See played a major role in assisting the victims of wars and natural famines. During my tenure as U.S. Ambassador, our embassy had frequent meetings with the leadership of the migration council on matters related to the refugees of Eastern Europe, Turkey, Lebanon, Albania, Ethiopia, Sudan, Southern Africa, and Vietnam. The Council is both the think tank and the action arena for the Pope on problems of migrants, homelessness, and people who are suffering because they have been separated from their traditional homeland.

The Gypsies

One matter that I took up with a junior member of the Pontifical Commission was the problem of the Gypsies in Europe. History books are full of folklore and stories about the Gypsies. Most of the countries in Southern and Eastern Europe have significant numbers. I was distressed because it was very difficult to find anyone in Europe who was sympathetic to the Gypsies. The average perception that a European or American has of a Gypsy in Europe is of a person using small children to beg and steal from local people, and especially from tourists. The use of children — very young children, sometime two to four years old — is especially distressing and automatically conveys a very negative image. It is true that the Gypsies have their own culture and traditions, and I never questioned the desirability of assisting these people to preserve those customs and traditions. But at one time, on a strictly personal basis with a member of the migration commission, I raised the desirability of the Church's doing something about modifying a behavioral pattern that results in a very negative perception to the outside world, that is, the Gypsies' tradition of employing children for the purposes of begging and stealing. I felt the commission should engage in a positive approach to behavioral modification with the hope that the conditions of the Gypsies would be greatly improved if they would to modify this behavioral pattern. While the commission was full of good intent in terms of protecting the rights of the Gypsies, they were not inclined to accept my advice on this matter.

I always discussed it personally so that my comment would not be regarded as official.

Cultural Treasures

On January 7, 1993, I participated in the opening of the Vatican exhibition "Rome Reborn" in the newly restored Southwest Gallery of the Library of Congress. Vatican treasures that had never left Rome were now on display at the Library of Congress. Two hundred items selected from some 150,000 bound manuscripts in the Vatican Library were there for many to see. They included Henry VIII's love letters, Galileo's sun-spot chart, and beautiful prints from the fifteenth and sixteenth centuries.

The Vatican Library, founded in the late fifteenth century in Rome, was the repository of the great works of literature, science, and art of that period.

This exhibit was a result of an exchange program that involved the Vatican Library, the Library of Congress, and the U.S. Embassy to the Holy See. I had started working on this project soon after my appointment in 1989, and it was a thrill to participate in the opening in Washington toward the end of my tenure in January of 1993.

The existence of full diplomatic relations between United States and the Holy See, which started only in 1984, makes if possible to work together in many positive endeavors, including the cultural.

The first U.S. Ambassador to the Holy See, William A. Wilson, and his wife Betty played a major role in developing the interest of Americans in the museums of the Vatican. Leading art specialists from all parts of the world advised the Vatican on restoration activities in the Sistine Chapel.

The opening night at the Library of Congress in 1993 brought together over one hundred fifty leaders of American cultural and educational organizations to view the role that the Holy See had played five hundred years before in preserving the records and the culture of that important era in the history of the world.

While the major emphasis of the U.S.-Holy See relationships was focused on human rights, religious freedom, and humanitarian affairs, there were frequent cultural contacts during the period of my tenure in Rome. The Sistine Chapel, the Vatican Library, the Art Collection, and the Museum are all priceless manifestations of the culture of the Christian world that the Vatican has so carefully preserved. Justice, humanitarian affairs, refugees, education, and cultural activities are all areas where the Holy See and the United States have a convergence of interest. The role of the Holy See is to set forth its position on these matters. In the case of the arts, books, and other works, it has played a major role in preserving them for all society.

I was pleasantly surprised at the great importance the Holy See gives to culture and the preservation of art, literature, and music of ages past. This is a very active program, making masterpieces now in the possession of the Vatican available to the world. The "Rome Reborn" exhibit in the United States in 1993 was part of this program.

The Holy See wants to encourage an interest in the arts as a means of maintaining a higher civilized tonal quality in world affairs. In my many talks with Vatican officials, it was evident that the excessive hedonism, escapism, vulgarity, and materialism in the world concern them because they view this as a degeneration of society. A positive reaction of their concern has been the important place they give to the role of culture, of art, music, and literature in our daily lives.

CHAPTER XII

The Holy See and the United States: The Future Relationships

THE SPECIAL positions in world affairs of the United States and the Holy See give them unique opportunities to collaborate in moderating many of the world's problems as we enter a new century.

The long, dark period of superpower confrontation is over. Eastern Europe and the Soviet Union have been liberated from the evils of an authoritarian communist system. The total failure of communism was very evident in the difficulties of these countries to develop a standard of living that approached that of the free-market countries. And the inability of the communist system to provide a decent standard of living was matched by a significant absence of guarantees for human rights and religious freedom in countries where communists controlled the government.

The end of the Soviet Union and its superpower status meant both the end of superpower confrontation and, for the most part, greater freedom in the countries that sprang from the old Soviet Union. These countries are developing guarantees that will protect human rights and religious freedom.

But while the dangers of superpower confrontation have ended, regional conflicts in the Balkans, the Caucasus, parts of Africa, and Asia are continuing to produce bloodshed, suffering, and death.

The sweep of independence in the 1960s and the '70s in Africa brought freedom from foreign domination. But most of these same countries are still plagued by the triple curse of poverty, illiteracy, and disease. Many of the African governments are authoritarian and have poor records as far as human rights are concerned.

On a broader scale, the gap in standard of living between the industrial countries of the north and the developing countries of the south continues to grow. The moral obscenity and the political dangers of this situation should be obvious to everyone.

All this and the emergence of the U.S. as the leading superpower coincided with the impact on world affairs of instant communications and the end of significant geographic distance. As natural and man-made disasters struck the peoples of Sudan, Ethiopia, Somalia, Liberia, Bangladesh, and Southern Africa, we knew about them almost immediately. And the United States and the Holy See worked together along with other countries and the United Nations to bring relief to the peoples there. Cooperation on humanitarian affairs helping millions of people was a clear benefit of the new closer diplomatic relationship between the United States and the Holy See.

The 1980s provided numerous instances of convergences in the interests of the United States and the Holy See. The central struggle was against the evil empire of communism. This battle was won! The cooperation in the 1980s between the Holy See and the United States was also assisted by the compatible positions of Presidents Reagan and Bush with the papal positions on abortion, school choice, and other moral matters. The Holy See has historically advocated the application of the Christian message on life from conception to death. It also has always advocated that parents should be able to have their tax dollars used to support their children in private and parochial schools. While there was significant opposition to these positions within the United States during the twelve years of the Reagan and Bush administrations, the two presidents themselves personally concurred and generally advocated positions that converged with the policies of the Holy See.

The administration of President Clinton, starting in 1993, sharply diverged from these policies. President Clinton essentially supports abortion on demand and is opposed to the support by government funds of parents to send their children to private or parochial schools.

These differences were dramatically portrayed in the visit of Pope John Paul II to Denver for World Youth Day in August 1993. Once with President Clinton at his side, and later in the closing hours of his visit in the presence of Vice President Gore, the Pope set forth in very clear terms his strong condemnation of abortion.

This presents a more complicating situation for U.S.-Holy See diplomatic cooperation. Presidents Reagan and Bush were respected as leaders of high moral commitment. It is not clear now what the long-term attitude of the Pope and his colleagues will be toward an administration that so strongly supports social policies that the Holy See considers seriously wrong.

Furthermore, there was generally more sympathy in the Reagan and Bush administrations for the traditional Judeo-Christian cultural heritage than there seems to be in the Clinton administration. On the other hand, the Clinton Administration is deeply committed to a strong social-justice agenda. Many Catholics in 1992 voted for Mr. Clinton because of his record on social-justice issues.

An apparent goal of the Clinton administration is to emphasize the numerous areas of convergence on international issues and to publicly ignore the differences on abortion. This was obvious during the visit of Pope John Paul II to Denver in 1993. President Clinton and Vice President Gore listened to the Pope's strong statements against abortion. They avoided the issue and in their public statements praised the Pope for his support of international social-justice causes.

The opportunities for convergence between the Holy See and the United States may be diminishing on the domestic scene. On the worldwide scene, however, the opportunities for convergence are dramatically increasing.

There is no question that the world is a better place without the dangers of a nuclear confrontation between the two superpowers. But regional conflicts are now growing. The future of Southern Africa is precarious. China, Iraq, Libya, Sudan, etc., still present many challenges in the area of human rights.

Peace in the Middle East is still not certain. Unfortunately, there will continue to be many man-made and natural disasters occurring in the world.

The Holy See, with its universal network and its moral commitment, and the United States, as the only real superpower in the world, can be effective collaborators on the world scene in promoting human rights, religious freedom, and the alleviation of human suffering.

The Pope as head of the Holy See and his colleagues in the government of the Holy See will continue to teach as they always have. This will include the full panorama of issues ranging from personal morality to questions of social justice in the world. It will be easier if the Holy See agrees with the fundamental direction of the national and international policies of the United States government. This was essentially true in the Reagan and Bush administrations. There was also greater convergence on international political issues during the administrations of Presidents Reagan and Bush because of the emphasis on winning the battle against the evil of worldwide communism. That goal has been reached and no longer offers a focus of convergence.

The challenge facing us now is to maintain this vital and very important cooperation that diplomatic relations facilitate on an international basis. Some people in the United States object when the Pope or the Holy See or its agencies speak out on such matter as abortion, parental rights in education, and other moral matters. The right of the Pope to speak on these matters should be protected, as this is his unique role in the world. The Pope will continue to speak on moral matters and will be universal in his application of the teaching. He will not be selective in his criticism!

The future holds such great challenges that the diplomatic relations between the Holy See and the United States should be strengthened. There is every indication that the relations may become more complicated. But the benefit of maintaining and strengthening these relationships is that millions of people in the world would normally benefit when the United States and the Holy See collaborate, together and with The United Nations, in strengthening and pushing the cause of human rights and religious freedom.

Now that the relationship may be more complicated, while at the same time offering greater opportunities, it is important that the relationship be regarded as very serious business. This means that on both sides of the relationship, the Holy See and the United States should appoint serious, competent personnel to their respective diplomatic positions. Temptations to use the positions for anything besides diplomacy between the two powers should be completely avoided.

There may be disagreements on the approach to solving problems, and sometimes even on substantive matters. But the greater common good calls for the United States and the Holy See to continue closer diplomatic cooperation, as there are so many people in the world who would benefit from this cooperation.

In the end there will be the judgment in favor of continued and expanded cooperation between the United States — the only major superpower in the world — and the Holy See — the only moral power with a worldwide constituency that has a government. So much good resulted from the first decade of diplomatic cooperation. And so much more can be done in the decades ahead for the human family, with improved communications and with the end of great geographic distance.

New successes can be achieved in the area of greater human rights and religious freedom for all, and more effective responses can be orchestrated to assist the victims of man-made and natural disasters.

The international community, especially the oppressed and less fortunate peoples, will benefit from a strong bilateral relationship between the United States and the Holy See. Since 1984, Old Glory and the Cross have maintained a mature, cooperative relationship. A careful nurturing of this relationship will benefit the world community.

APPENDIX I

Author's Note on the Government of the Holy See

The Government of the United States has diplomatic relations with the government of the Roman Catholic Church; that is, the Holy See. The 1984 U.S. recognition of the Holy See as a sovereign personality in the world community of states included the understanding by the United States Senate that the official U.S. government relationship would be with those aspects of the Holy See government that were appropriate for the United States in accordance with the American Constitution and traditions.

These included the diplomatic activities of the Holy See, those offices that obtain information on governmental, political, and diplomatic matters from all parts of the world, and those offices which carry out the Pope's public-policy missions especially as related to human rights, religious freedom, and humanitarian affairs.

Also included was contact with the papal agencies responsible for developing societies, refugees and migrants, health matters, and environmental concerns.

The 1984 recognition by the United States also implicitly noted that there were activities of the Holy See that were not appropriate matters for U.S. government involvement. These included religious doctrine, appointments of bishops, canonization of saints, and Church regulations on moral and ethical matters like abortion and euthanasia.

A. The Holy See: Government of the Catholic Church

The Holy See is the composite of the authority, jurisdiction, and sovereignty vested in and exercised by the Pope and his advisers in the temporal and spiritual direction and guidance of the Roman Catholic Church throughout the world. The Holy See, consequently, is a moral entity; in modern terms, it is the central government of the Roman Catholic Church. As such, the Holy See is an institution which, under international law and in practice, has a legal identity which allows it to enter into treaties as the juridical equal of a state, and to send and receive diplomatic representatives. The Holy See has formal diplomatic relations with over 144 nations, including the United States. This world-wide body has over 900 million members.

Representatives of the Holy See to states have the title of Nuncio. This is the Vatican's title for Ambassador. When there are no diplomatic ties to a country, the Pope normally has an Apostolic Delegate, who is his representative with the local bishops.

The Pope's Ambassador has two functions. One is diplomatic as an ambassador of the Holy See to the government where he is accredited. The other is religious, as a representative to the local church of the Pope to assure that canonical regulations are being followed. He also recommends appointments of new bishops. When there are no diplomatic relations, the Pope's representative has solely a religious role.

Vatican City State is the physical seat of the Holy See. The Holy See is a sovereign entity that has this unique universal sovereignty because of the role of the Pope of the Catholic Church in the world. The Holy See is subject to international law, sends and receives diplomatic envoys, and has all other rights of sovereignty. The relationship of Vatican City/State to the sovereignty of the Holy See is like that of Washington, D.C., to the U.S.A. Both Vatican City and Washington, D.C. serve as seats of their respective governments.

B. Government and Institutions

The Pope exercises supreme legislative, executive, and judicial power over the Holy See. He is the equivalent of an absolute monarch. This authority is not restricted to the State of Vatican City. The sovereignty of the Holy See is a universal historical fact accepted by international society. The Holy See has sent and received diplomatic missions since the fourth century. The Pope rules the Holy See through the Roman Curia and the Papal Civil Service which staffs it.

The Roman Curia consists of the Secretariat of State with its two sections: General Affairs, and Relations with States; nine Congregations, (equivalent to Ministries), three Tribunals, eleven Councils, and a complex of Commissions, Secretariats, and Offices which administer Church affairs at the highest level. The Curia is directed and coordinated by the Secretariat of State, under the Secretary of State, who is the Holy See's second-ranking official and is the equivalent of Prime Minister. The Secretary for Relations with States is — in effect — the Vatican's

Foreign Minister. Most of the contacts of the U.S. Embassy are with this office.

C. The Roman Curia

The government is outlined below as it was in place during my tour of duty as Ambassador.

The congregations, tribunals, councils, offices, commissions, and institutions in italics are the ones with which my staff and I would be in official contact. The others not in italics are the ones where the embassy had little official contact because they were primarily religious — Church operations of the Holy See.

Secretariat of State (Secretary of State)

First Section: Section for General Affairs (*Sostituto*, Substitute Secretary of State)

Second Section: Section for Relations with States (Substitute Secretary, Undersecretary)

Congregations

Congregation for the Doctrine of the Faith (Prefect)

Congregation for the Oriental Churches (Prefect)

Congregation for Divine Worship and the Discipline of the Sacraments (Prefect)

Congregation for the Causes of Saints (Prefect)

Congregation for Bishops (Prefect)

Pontifical Commission for Latin America (Prefect)

Congregation for the Evangelization of Peoples (Prefect)

Congregation for the Clergy (Prefect)

Pontifical Commission for Preserving the Patrimony of Art and History (Secretary)

Congregation for Institutes of Consecrated Life and for Societies of Apostolic Life (Prefect)

Congregation for Catholic Education (Prefect)

Standing Interdicasterial Commission for Clergy Distribution (President)

Tribunals

Apostolic Penitentiary (Major Penitentiary)

Supreme Tribunal of the Apostolic Signatura (Pro-Prefect)

Tribunal of the Roman Rota (Dean)

Pontifical Councils

Pontifical Council for the Laity (President)

Pontifical Council for Promoting Christian Laity (President)

Commission for Religious Relations with Jews (President)

Pontifical Council for the Family (President)

Pontifical Council for Justice and Peace (President)

Pontifical Council "Cor Unum" (President)

Pontifical Council for the Pastoral Care of Migrants and Itinerant Peoples (President)

Pontifical Council for Pastoral Assistance to Health Care Workers (President)

Pontifical Council for the Interpretation of Legislative Texts (President)

Pontifical Council for Interreligious Dialogue (President)

Pontifical Council for Dialogue with Non-Believers (President)

Pontifical Council for Culture (President)

Pontifical Council for Social Communications (President)

Offices

Apostolic Camera (Chamberlain of the Holy Roman Church)

Administration of the Patrimony of the Holy See (President)

Prefecture for the Economic Affairs of the Holy See (President)

Prefecture of the Papal Household (Prefect)

Office for the Liturgical Celebrations of the Supreme Pontiff
(Master of Ceremonies)

Commissions and Committees

Pontifical Biblical Commission (President)

International Theological Commission (President)

Pontifical Committee for International Eucharistic Congresses
(President)

Pontifical Commission of Sacred Archaeology (President)

Pontifical Committee of Historical Sciences (President)

Pontifical Commission "Ecclesia Dei" (President)

Disciplinary Commission of the Roman Curia (President)

Institutions Connected with the Holy See

Vatican Secret Archives (Pro-Archivist)

Vatican Apostolic Library (Pro-Librarian)

Pontifical Academy of Sciences (President)

Vatican Radio (President of the Coordinating Committee)

Vatican Television Centre (President of the Administrative Council)

Fabric of Saint Peter's (President)

Office of Papal Charities (Almoner)

Vatican Polyglot Press (Director General, Administrative Director)

Vatican Publishing House (President)

Institute for Works of Religion (Prelate)

L'Osservatore Romano (Editor-in-Chief)

Press Office of the Holy See (Director)

APPENDIX II

Hearings on the Opening of a U.S. Embassy

Hearing

Before the

Committee of Foreign Relations

United States Senate

on nomination of

William A. Wilson

to be

Ambassador to the Holy See

February 2, 1984

[*The Committee announced before the Hearings that their deliberations would focus on the question: should the United States have diplomatic relations with the Holy See? These hearings subsequently were not primarily to examine the credentials of Mr. Wilson. A vote favoring Mr. Wilson was a vote in favor of diplomatic relations. The vote was 15 in favor and 1 opposed.*]

NOMINATION OF WILLIAM A. WILSON

THURSDAY, FEBRUARY 2, 1984

UNITED STATES SENATE,

COMMITTEE ON FOREIGN RELATIONS,

Washington, D.C.

The committee met, pursuant to notice, at 2:31 p.m., in room SD-419, Dirksen Senate Office Building, Hon. Richard Lugar presiding.

Present: Senators Lugar, Percy, Helms, Mathias, Murkowski, Pell, and Tsongas.

Senator LUGAR. This meeting of the Foreign Relations Committee for the purpose of hearing the nomination of William A. Wilson of California to be Ambassador to the Holy See is now called to order.

It is the pleasure of the Chair to recognize the distinguished junior Senator from the State of California, Pete Wilson, to make the introduction of the nominee.

STATEMENT OF HON. PETE WILSON, A U.S. SENATOR FROM CALIFORNIA

Senator WILSON. Thank you very much, Mr. Chairman, for giving me the privilege of introducing to you a fellow Californian, a very distinguished American and public servant. I would love to tell you yet another member of the far-flung Wilson clan, but I cannot, though, after diligent search find any blood relationship to the nominee, and I have certainly tried. I am very proud, however, to be able to claim him as a friend.

Mr. Chairman, in the interest of the committee's time and that of the nominee, I will try to come quickly to the point. There will, I assume, be witnesses who follow me and who follow the nominee wishing to address the committee with respect to what they term the propriety or lack of propriety of an action that I would point out is an accomplished fact.

Diplomatic relations were established between the United States and the Vatican as of January 10 of this year. The establishment of diplomatic relations with the Vatican simply took into account the reality that the Holy See is in many respects a world power with great influence upon the opinions and the lives of a great many people throughout the world and, in particular, in areas where vital American interests are at stake.

I mention that not to excite counterargument. That probably will not be necessary. But I would point out that the action has been taken. That debate has occurred in Congress and the decision has been taken. So what we are concerned with, quite properly, today, Mr. Chairman, is not the propriety of this relationship. The relationship exists.

What we are concerned with are the credentials of the nominee and for that reason I am very happy to turn to those credentials because they are outstanding. There are two reasons why William Wilson should be the U.S. Ambassador to the Vatican.

The first is that he is an outstanding public servant. His own personal record, even on a rather modest biography, makes clear that he has been an outstanding citizen. He has served his Nation in more than one capacity, in the armed services, and also he has served as the personal representative of the President of the United States to the Holy See for the past three years.

That, of course, is the second and even more pertinent reason. It is because of his experience these past three years that he has a special insight into the relationship existing. This is not experience which I think anyone else is able to duplicate.

He has been an outstanding member of his community, serving as a civic activist in a variety of capacities. He is interested and involved in educational, health, and cultural activities that are too numerous to mention. He has been recognized by foreign governments for his service. Most notably, he has received the Gold Medal of the Italian Red Cross this past year, as just one indication of the outstanding career which he has had and particularly in the past three years.

No one, I submit, has had a better education, a better preparation for the responsibilities of the American Ambassador to the Holy See than has William Wilson. He knows the problems, knows the opportunities. He comes to today's hearings with the greatest eagerness to perform the new responsibility that will be his now that diplomatic relations have in fact been restored with the Holy See.

Mr. Chairman, rather than go on at greater length, I will simply say that it is a privilege for me to support this nomination, not only because I do count Bill Wilson as a personal friend but because I think that his service to his Nation and in this particular responsibility is one for which he is not only admirably suited but more suited than any other person who might have been brought forward as a nominee.

So with that I respectfully urge that the committee confirm the President's appointment. It is one that will reflect great credit on this administration and great credit upon the United States.

I thank you, Mr. Chairman, for the opportunity.

Senator LUGAR. Thank you very much, Senator Wilson, for that eloquent introduction.

Let me outline the agenda for the hearing. We want the hearing to be complete and thorough, and for all points of view to be heard in the course of the afternoon. I will make an opening statement. I will then recognize Senator Percy, the distinguished chairman of our committee, who may have an opening statement, then Senator Tsongas at that point, and then the nominee for his statement. And then Senators will question the nominee until their questions are satisfied.

At that time, the nominee will be excused from the witness table and the committee will hear from two panels of individuals who are coming forward to testify either on the nominee himself or on the whole proposition of having an Ambassador to the Holy See. We will hear all of those witnesses today and committee members will have an opportunity to question both panels.

We will hope in this way to have as complete a record as possible.

Let me say at the outset that the Foreign Relations Committee meets today to hear the President's nominee to be Ambassador to the Holy See. The committee welcomes Mr. William Wilson, who has served ably for the past three years as the President's personal envoy to the Holy See.

I believe the President has made a wise decision in establishing diplomatic relations with the Holy See and in nominating William Wilson to conduct those relations at the ambassadorial level.

The Holy See maintains a diplomatic presence and has wide influence and unique access in areas of great concern to the foreign policy of the United States. Eastern Europe, Central America, Africa, and the Philippines offer excellent examples.

Vatican officials and diplomats are not simply observers or moral guides but play an active role in international affairs. A prominent recent example is the successful papal mediation of the Beagle Channel dispute between Argentina and Chile, a problem which for a century had defied resolution.

Over the past two years, the President, the Vice President, the Secretary of State, and other Cabinet officers have had audiences with the Pope to discuss a wide range of political and moral problems which confront the world. Every President of the United States in recent memory has indicated his respect for the prominent international standing of the Papacy by meeting with the Pope.

The Vatican is deeply involved in issues of vital importance to the United States such as Poland and Lebanon. Less well known, perhaps, but equally important are the many other issues upon which the U.S. government works on a day-to-day basis with the Vatican. Immigration policy, refugee resettlement, food and medicine distribution, and a host of other activities comprise the business of normal working relationships between governments.

Last summer I had occasion to witness firsthand the importance of the Vatican on the modern political scene. I visited with the Pope, along with the distinguished chairman of this committee and other Senators, as part of a delegation to Europe to discuss issues of arms control and deployment of intermediate-range missiles.

Our visit came on the eve of the Pope's historic mission to Poland, where he has worked with great influence. Pope John Paul II is a powerful force for the political and moral values which we in the United States cherish and which are so important to the dignity of men and women everywhere.

Our representative to the Vatican handles a constant flow of requests from both the executive branch and the Congress on behalf of officials who wish to see the Pope or other Vatican officials — to discuss areas of mutual interest. The fact is that in many ways the Vatican is a far more significant and wide-ranging factor than many of the other governments with which we maintain formal relations.

This fact has been generally acknowledged by 107 other nations, including almost all of the major countries of the world, except the Soviet Union and the People's Republic of China. The Holy See has entered into international treaties, some of which have had the United States as cosignatories. In short, the Holy See is an internationally recognized sovereign entity and is represented at international organizations such as the United Nations and the Organization of American States.

For each of these reasons it is fitting and appropriate that we should send an Ambassador to the Holy See. The relationship is consistent not only with common sense but also with American tradition and with the practice of the early administrations of our Republic.

I will not argue the case further today. I will simply say I believe the burden of proof lies upon those who would argue that there is a special reason to abrogate the President's clearly stated constitutional authority to name Ambassadors. The President established diplomatic relations with the Holy See on January 10, 1984. Strictly speaking, Senators will be called upon not to judge this action but to judge the suitability of Mr. Wilson for the post for which he has been nominated.

However, because a number of individuals have expressed concern about the general question of the propriety of United States-Vatican relations, the committee has invited witnesses to speak to this question so that all Senators might have the benefit of their thoughts for a complete committee record. We will welcome these individuals presently.

Let me review for the benefit of the committee and the witness a chronology of events preceding this hearing. The late Clement Zablocki, chairman of the House Foreign Affairs Committee, introduced a resolution on June 30, 1983, to repeal the prohibition against funding of a delegation in Rome. His House bill had bipartisan cosponsorship from twenty-six Members of the House, including a majority of the members of the Foreign Affairs Committee.

I introduced a companion bill on August 3, 1983, and the bill that I introduced had bipartisan cosponsorship from twenty-three Senators. This measure was offered as an amendment to S. 1342, the State Department authorization bill, on September 22, 1983.

It was the third amendment considered. Consideration of the State Department bill, I might add, occurred on and off over a period of four weeks. In the midst of this consideration, opponents of the amendment that I had introduced held a national press conference on Capitol Hill on October 5.

Final passage of S. 1342 did not occur until October 20, a day on which the Senate considered twenty-nine first-degree amendments, with ample opportunity for any Senator to raise an objection or a question with regard to the amendment during consideration of the bill.

The Senate-House conference met on the State Department bill on November 1, 2, 3, 8, and 10. After discussion of the Senate amendment, the House receded and accepted the Senate position, and discussion was held in which several of us were engaged in an open session of that conference committee.

The State Department bill returned to both the Senate and the House. The Senate passed the conference report on November 18. No question was raised by any Senator about the Vatican amendment. The President signed the bill on November 22.

At each stage of the process, my office issued notice to the press about the progress of the legislation, and I took part in a number of media interviews on the subject during each stage. During the month of December the President considered, amid widespread press speculation, whether to proceed to establish formal diplomatic relations with the Holy See.

He determined that he should do so on January 10, 1984. Ambassador-Designate Wilson's nomination papers arrived with the customary request by the administration that the Senate consider the nomination in a timely fashion, which we are proceeding to do today.

Having made that opening statement, I would like to recognize now the nominee. Mr. Wilson, do you have an opening statement?

STATEMENT OF HON. WILLIAM A. WILSON, OF CALIFORNIA,

AMBASSADOR-DESIGNATE TO THE HOLY SEE

Mr. WILSON. Yes, Mr. Chairman, I do indeed.

First I would like to recognize you, Mr. Chairman, and the other members of the committee and to thank you for this opportunity to be here to present a statement and to answer questions.

I would also like to take the opportunity to thank my namesake from California, Senator Wilson, for his kind remarks and his introductory statement. Senator, thank you very much.

Senator WILSON. My pleasure.

Mr. WILSON. First let me say what a great honor it is for me to have been asked to serve my country and my President in this capacity — first in the capacity as personal envoy of the President of the United States to the Holy See, and now as an Ambassador to the Holy See. I want to assure you that if I am confirmed I will make every effort to do this job to the very best of my ability.

One question that undoubtedly will be asked is how the United States will derive more benefits from having full diplomatic or normal diplomatic relations with the Vatican over and above what we may have derived in the past. The answer to that question, I believe, will have a bit more meaning if I would be permitted a few minutes to review briefly the history of our relations with the papal states and with the Holy See from the beginning of time, which is 1797 until now.

I should point out that the first amendment to the Constitution, which often comes up for consideration in this regard, was enacted in 1791 and it was in 1797, in the last year of President Washington's term of office as President, that the United States sent the first consul to Rome, representing the United States to the papal states.

We maintained consular relations with the papal states from 1797 until 1848, at which time relations were upgraded to that of a legation in charge of a minister. From 1848 until 1867 we had four ministers serving our country in Rome, representing us to the papal states, each one of whom was confirmed by the Senate.

Indeed, the world situation has changed a great deal since 1867 and while the Popes and the papal states have lost some of their geography, some of their temporal domain, so to speak; they have indeed at the same time increased in world influence, moral assuasion, and in diplomatic presence.

I will not go into the remarks. I had some remarks that have been covered by not only my friend and namesake from California but also, Mr. Chairman, in your remarks. So a portion of the statement which I submit for the record I will skip. It has been covered.

I simply would like to say, however, that with respect to the question of the benefits to be derived from full diplomatic relations with the Vatican and with having a full Ambassador, they will be primarily derived from a permanent presence there — a permanence which has not been the case since 1867.

As you perhaps know, various Presidents from President Roosevelt until President Reagan have sent personal envoys; That has not been a continuous situation. There were three Presidents there that did not send a personal envoy, so it has been a discontinuous situation and one which does not tend to create a feeling of permanence between the two nations — that is, the United States and the Holy See.

So with a permanence and with a permanent office we would expect to develop better channels of communication by which both the United States and the Holy See will benefit.

I want to thank you very much, Mr. Chairman, for the opportunity to present these remarks, and I look forward to answering any questions that I may.

[Mr. Wilson's prepared statement follows:]

PREPARED STATEMENT OF HON. WILLIAM A. WILSON

Mr. Chairman, members of the committee, I am grateful to you and to the members of the Committee for the opportunity to appear before you today.

It is a great honor to have been asked to serve my country and the President in this important position. If confirmed, I assure you that I will do so to the best of my ability.

One might ask the question, how will the upgrading of our relations with the Vatican increase the benefits we gain from that relationship, as compared to the level of relations we formerly maintained? The answer to that question might have a bit more meaning if, with your permission, I spend a moment reviewing the history of the United States' relations with the former papal states.

The United States sent its first consul to Rome to represent the U.S. government in the capital of the papal states in 1797, the last year of President George Washington's term of office. We maintained consular relations with the papal states until 1848, when the relations were raised to the level of a legation headed by a Minister. From 1848 to 1867, four ministers represented our government to the papal states; all of the ministers were confirmed by the Senate.

The world situation has changed drastically since that time. Although the Popes lost their temporal domains, except for Vatican City in Rome, the importance of the Vatican in world affairs has increased enormously since those days. Recognizing this, the Congress last year acted to open the way for the President to reestablish normal diplomatic relations with the Holy See.

That legislation was introduced last June in the House by the late Congressman Zablocki and in the Senate by you, Mr. Chairman. The legislation was signed by the President in November and on December 15, 1983 after consultation with the Congress, and on instruction from the President, diplomatic notes were exchanged with the Vatican. Public announcement was made on January 10, 1984, thus establishing formal diplomatic relations between the United States government and the Holy See. We thereby joined 107 other countries which had already established such relations.

The next step is to send an Ambassador to the Holy See. Let me tell you why I think this step is so important to our national interest.

The Vatican is an important player in the world stage. It is a sovereign state and its influence is even more far-reaching today than during the nineteenth century, when we last maintained diplomatic relations.

The Vatican maintains a diplomatic presence and has wide influence and access to important areas of great interest to the United States, such as Eastern Europe, Central America, Africa, the Middle East, and the Philippines. Vatican diplomats, widely regarded as among the most skilled in the world, are not simply observers or moral guides, but play an active role in international political affairs.

To choose but one recent example, just this month, after years of patient diplomacy, it appears the Vatican is successfully mediating a solution to the century-old dispute over the Beagle Channel, which had threatened many times to drive Argentina and Chile to war.

Less well known, however, are the Vatican's day-to-day but very important activities related to issues across the whole spectrum of American concerns, including immigration policy, refugee resettlement, food and medicine distribution, narcotics control, education, and many more.

Thus, the Vatican influences a whole range of issues important to U.S. foreign-policy interests. While our views do not always coincide, the United States can only derive benefit from the improved exchange of insights afforded by upgrading our relations. Sending an Ambassador to the Holy See would be an expression of our intention to maintain the closest possible diplomatic relations with this small but influential sovereign state.

In sum, I believe that having a permanent embassy and a full-time ambassador accredited to the Vatican will enhance our ability to make sure that the Vatican understands the U.S. government's position on the vital issues of the day. The Vatican is in many respects a world power and it is in our best foreign policy interests to treat it accordingly.

I thank you for this opportunity to appear before you and to make comments and I will be pleased to respond to your questions. Thank you.

Senator LUGAR. Thank you, Mr. Wilson.

As a matter of common consent we will proceed with a ten-minute time limit on the first round by Senators. Senators have, I understand, combinations of questions and statements, and if we can proceed in this manner it would be the Chair's intent to recognize first Senator Percy, then Senator Pell, then Senator Murkowski, then Senator Tsongas, and then any additional Senators that may come in.

Without objection, we will proceed in that way. The Chair recognizes the distinguished chairman of the Foreign Relations Committee, Senator Percy of Illinois.

The CHAIRMAN. Thank you, Senator Lugar, very much.

Mr. Wilson, I have received a great deal of mail, as you would undoubtedly expect, on the President's decision to establish formal diplomatic relations with the Vatican. For this committee, however, the issue is your qualifications to be an Ambassador to the Holy See.

The issue as to whether or not the President has the authority to name an Ambassador to the Holy See has been settled by the Congress.

I cannot recall a single letter against you personally for the post. Rather, the letters have dealt with the principle of church-state separation and whether we should have formal relations with the Vatican. Therefore, I will address my questions mainly to those issues.

My own personal observation is that you are superbly qualified for this post.

The first question that was raised in so many letters is what would be your focus of activities and duties as Ambassador to the Holy See and would you differentiate between the Pope as chief of state of Vatican City and as leader of the Roman Catholic Church?

Mr. WILSON. Yes, Senator Percy. First I want to thank you for your nice comments concerning my personal qualifications. It was very nice to hear and very gratifying.

Let me take the first question first — the focus of activities at my post in Rome. The activities are varied. They vary from attempting to explain and clarify the position of the United States in various foreign policy matters to the appropriate people in the Vatican and from there then to arranging visits of various people from our Government to the Holy See, to the Vatican.

As the chairman mentioned a little while ago, we have arranged visits for the President, the Vice President, two Secretaries of State, Secretary of Defense, Attorney General, and on and on. Those are not the essential aspects of the position, however. The essential aspect of the position is really to work with the Vatican in explaining and clarifying to them our position in foreign policy.

If I can use an example, one of the first responsibilities that I undertook when I went over there was, after a rather full briefing on Central America here in our State Department, to explain to the people in the Vatican what our goals were in Central America, how we were hopeful of accomplishing those goals, and to discuss with them how our position and what we were trying to do fitted in with what they would like to try to accomplish down there from a moral standpoint.

We had other discussions of a similar nature with respect to Poland, with respect to the Middle East, particularly the Lebanon situation, in late months, and also in certain areas of Africa. We even have had discussions concerning China.

With respect to the distinction of the Pope with respect to the political body, the governing body of the City of the Vatican state and the church, the Pope is the head of the Vatican City-State as a separate sovereign entity, a separate sovereign country.

He is also the head of the Roman Catholic Church in a situation very similar to the situation in England where the Queen or the reigning head is the head of the Anglican Church, and at the same time head of the Government of the British Empire.

The CHAIRMAN. Thank you. What would be the principal differences between serving as a personal representative of the President and that of being an Ambassador, so far as U.S. diplomatic relations with the Vatican are concerned?

Mr. WILSON. The primary difference is the difference between permanence and nonpermanence. As the personal envoy of the President starting in 1939 when President Roosevelt sent Mr. Myron Taylor over there until the present day, we have had either a temporary situation or no situation. Mr. Taylor did indeed spend quite a bit of time in Rome. I think he had an apartment, and I think his apartment served as the office part of the time.

But he was not there full time, nor have any of the personal representatives from Presidents since that time. They have spent a few weeks and then returned to the United States. They did not, as I understand it, give up their business relationships. My immediate predecessor, Robert Wagner, continued his legal practice in New York, for example.

The difference, then, would be that if an Ambassador is sent there, if I am confirmed, I will spend full time; I have not been spending full time; I have been spending six or seven months a year over there. One of the purposes behind that was that I did not want it to appear as though I were something I really was not. So for that reason I have spent less than full time.

With an Ambassador we would have a permanence of presence over there which then establishes confidence in those with whom you deal in the Vatican and will result in a much better exchange of communications.

The CHAIRMAN. From our standpoint, the difference is that for the first time since 1867 the Senate has oversight and confirmation responsibilities and would be able to learn more officially about your performance and the important issues with which you may be concerned.

Would you pledge to this committee that for the entire period that you serve as Ambassador that you will make yourself available to testify personally before this committee, to make this committee aware of all of the activities that you undertake, and that you will be fully and completely candid with this committee, even in classified sessions, as to the nature and range of your activities as Ambassador to the Holy See?

Mr. WILSON. I certainly do so pledge.

The CHAIRMAN. This will be the first time since President Roosevelt sent a personal representative to the Vatican in 1939 that we will have the advantage of oversight responsibility as well as information.

Mr. WILSON. That is my understanding and I so pledge.

The CHAIRMAN. Let me draw from some of the letters that I have received. The opponents of the President's decision to establish formal diplomatic relations with the Holy See contend that it may violate the first amendment of the Constitution which states that "Congress shall make no law respecting the establishment of religion or prohibiting the free exercise thereof."

Even if it does not violate the Constitution, critics contend that at the very least it violates the American tradition of separation of church and state. What is your personal view on these two criticisms of the President's decision to establish formal diplomatic relations with the Vatican, and do formal diplomatic relations confer on the Roman Catholic Church any preferential status over other religious denominations in the United States, be it Judaism, Christianity, Islam, whatever?

Mr. WILSON. With respect to the first question, the separation of church and state, as may have been provided for by the first amendment, first let me reply by saying that I am not an attorney, so I am not really capable of interpreting the first amendment.

However, I would suggest that as I mentioned in my opening remarks, General Washington sent the first consular representative of the United States to the papal states within six years after the enactment of the first amendment, so it would seem clear to me. But, again, I say I am not an attorney.

It would seem to me that the intent of the first amendment in the minds of those who had the responsibility for writing and enacting it certainly did not preclude sending a diplomatic representative to the papal states.

Were you going to ask a question?

The CHAIRMAN. No; go ahead.

Mr. WILSON. Second, with respect to the relation between the Government of the United States and the Catholic Church, the Roman Catholic Church and the United States, I can assure you, I can assure everybody here, that the relationship between those two bodies will in no way change as a result of this relationship.

The CHAIRMAN. Finally, will the United States have the same relationship with the Vatican as do 107 other countries, including Yugoslavia, whose President just had luncheon with us? Will it be helpful in areas of peace where the Holy See has taken a very active role? Might this strengthen our relationships in such a way that it could hopefully advance somewhat the cause of peace in the world?

Mr. WILSON. Indeed I do, Senator Percy. True peace, true peace — which is not just the absence of war, but true peace — is living together in peace and unity. It really comes from understanding, and understanding comes from dialog, and dialog comes from being able to exchange ideas.

I do think that our establishing relationships with the Holy See would indeed give us a better means of communication, a better understanding particularly in those areas of the world that have caused us problems in the past and may still be causing us problems. I think I am referring not only to the Middle East and Central America and some of the places we read about, but in general the Eastern bloc countries.

The CHAIRMAN. Thank you very much.

Mr. WILSON. Thank you.

The CHAIRMAN. My best wishes to you and your family.

Mr. WILSON. Thank you very much.

Senator LUGAR. Thank you very much, Mr. Chairman.

The Chair would like to now recognize the distinguished ranking minority member of the committee, Senator Claiborne Pell of Rhode Island.

Senator PELL. Thank you, Mr. Chairman.

I have felt for many years that the United States national interest would be advanced by having a formal relationship with the Vatican and its excellent diplomatic service.

The nominee and I were chatting about this the other day in my office, but I would like to bring up publicly this question of his opinion of the sophistication and the knowledge of the Vatican officials and how we can benefit from their advice, because I think there is no country or no government — and it is a government in its own — that has had more experience in dealing with the communist world and keeping religious ideas alive behind the Curtain, with the exception of Lithuania and Czechoslovakia, where things are very grim, but in other parts of Eastern Europe where the Roman Catholic Church and the Vatican have been very successful in dealing with the Communists.

I would hope that you would make yourself available to Cardinal Casaroli, the Secretary of State there, and relay his advice and suggestions and thoughts to our own Government. Would that be your intention, sir?

Mr. WILSON. Yes, indeed, Senator Pell. It is my intention and I have attempted to do that in the past. I have met, as we mentioned the other day, many times with Cardinal Casaroli, with Monsignor Backis, with Monsignor Silvestrini, and with others in their Secretariat of State who are familiar with problems in the Eastern bloc countries that you mentioned. And indeed the situation in Czechoslovakia is grim and dim.

Senator PELL. Won't you have more of an opportunity of exchanging ideas and learning their views as an Ambassador than you do have as the personal representative?

Mr. WILSON. Absolutely, and this is the point that I think is very important, that with the permanence of an ambassadorship and the permanence of full diplomatic relations, normal diplomatic relations, they will have more confidence in us and will exchange information with us more freely and with this I will be able to report back to the State Department, back to our Government, on how we can work better with them and other governments to try to develop this dialog and understanding — a mutual understanding — so that we can work toward peace in the world and coexistence.

Senator PELL. And as an Ambassador you will have the right of access to the Chief of State of the Holy See.

Mr. WILSON. That is correct, Senator; yes.

Senator PELL. When you were personal representative you were accredited also to the Holy See, not to the Vatican, correct?

Mr. WILSON. I did present a letter of introduction to the Holy Father when I first went over there in 1981. I will now have official — that was sort of the courtesy situation. Now we have an official situation.

Senator PELL. Then the biographical sheet here which says that your present rank or title is that of Personal Representative of the President to the Holy See is not correct. You are really Personal Representative of the President to the Holy Father; is that correct? So that should be corrected?

Mr. WILSON. Yes; I think that is probably more accurate.

Senator PELL. One other point is you will actually be the first Ambassador in our history because the previous representative we had were Ministers before, and, as you know, a Minister represents the Chief, the Ministry of Foreign Relations, or the Secretary of State. You represent in your person the Chief of State or the President, so in a sense this is a promotion, and I am glad of it. I believe in it.

Mr. WILSON. Thank you very much. If confirmed, I would in fact become our first Ambassador to the Holy See.

Senator PELL. A couple of details here. I am just curious. When it comes to the Vatican's representative, the Holy See's representation here in Washington, will they be represented by a nuncio, an internuncio, a pronuncio? What will they be represented by?

Mr. WILSON. My understanding is they will be represented by a pronuncio, which is the Latin definition of an Ambassador from the Vatican; however, an Ambassador who will not automatically take up a position as dean of the diplomatic corps in Washington.

Senator PELL. And if he was an internuncio he would then be the rank of Minister; would that be correct?

Mr. WILSON. That is right; the Holy See's rank of internuncio does in fact equate to the diplomatic rank of Minister.

Senator PELL. If he is just a straight nuncio he would be dean of the diplomatic corps automatically. That is why he is called a pronuncio.

Mr. WILSON. That is correct; if he were nuncio and the United States had a treaty with the Holy See according him the position of dean. However, we do not have such an agreement.

Senator PELL. I also notice that with your direct access you will be able to take up questions immediately with the Pope, with the Holy Father when you wish.

Mr. WILSON. Yes; that is my understanding and my hope.

Senator PELL. Even arranging in even more rapid style than you have for appointments for itinerant Members of Congress. [Laughter.]

I noticed also that you have amongst your memberships the Knights of Malta. Do you see any conflict of interest there? As you know, they also claim to be a sovereign entity and they also appoint Ambassadors to about twenty or twenty-five different countries.

Mr. WILSON. That is correct.

Senator PELL. So in a sense you will have an Ambassador of your own. Do you see any conflict there?

Mr. WILSON. Being a member of the Knights of Malta does not make me a citizen of their country.

Senator PELL. Nobody is a citizen of the Knights of Malta, but you are a member of the Knights themselves, with Ambassadors accredited to about twenty different countries.

Mr. WILSON. Yes. It is not a conflict; I can assure you.

Senator PELL. Thank you very much.

Mr. WILSON. Thank you.

Senator LUGAR. Thank you very much, Senator Pell.

The Chair would like to now recognize Senator Murkowski of Alaska.

Senator MURKOWSKI. Thank you very much, Mr. Chairman. I appreciate this opportunity. I speak on behalf of the nominee, William Wilson. I think it is clear to all of us that Pope John Paul has dedicated himself to the cause of world peace. From Poland to the tip of South America, the Pope has brought an element of stability and hope to the many troubled regions of the world.

Mr. Chairman, I am going to depart from the questions and just read this brief statement because I think most of mine have been answered.

I believe it is because of the Pope's influence and impact that it is in the best interest of this country to establish full diplomatic relations with the Holy See. Mr. Chairman, we are not recognizing a particular religion but instead are enhancing a diplomatic avenue for the advancement of peace and stability in the world.

As you have said, Mr. Wilson, over one hundred nations have seen that close ties with the Holy See are in their best interest and really the interests of the world as a whole.

Opponents of the concept and this nomination contend that it violates America's historic adherence to the separation of church and state embodied in the — first amendment to the Constitution. Although popular discussions frequently utilize that Jeffersonian metaphor of the wall of separation between church and state, the Supreme Court's reading of the clause has never approached that degree of absoluteness.

To quote the Court: "The judicial caveats against entanglement must recognize that the line of separation, far from being a wall, is a blurred, indistinct barrier, depending on all the circumstances of the particular relationship."

Indeed, it can be argued that it is neutrality that the Constitution mandates, not separation. Opponents also express their concern that we are bestowing some special status on the Catholic Church, yet it is not certainly apparent to this Senator how this move involves the United States in any religious activity.

The principal evils that must be avoided, of course, are sponsorship and financial support, and they are certainly not visible in this relationship. The aim of establishing diplomatic relations with the Holy See is not to advance religious causes but to advance U.S. foreign policy interests around the globe. The purpose and effect of full diplomatic relations with the Holy See is indeed secular in nature.

In conclusion, Mr. Chairman, with the state of international relations as tense as they are now, I believe we must make better use of the Pope's influence as a mediator of international crises. To do otherwise is to fail to utilize all the tools of the diplomatic trade which are within our grasp.

Thank you, Mr. Chairman.

Senator LUGAR. Thank you very much, Senator Murkowski. Is Senator Tsongas going to return for questions? Will you please check?

Mr. WILSON. Do we have a moment, Mr. Chairman? I would like, if I may, to introduce the members of my family that are here. Right behind me is Mrs. Wilson. If she would stand I would appreciate it.

My wife and my daughter, Marsha Hobbs. Thank you very much, Mr. Chairman.

Senator LUGAR. We are very pleased to have the members of your family here today.

I see no other Senators who wish to raise questions. As is already evident, I support the President's right to proceed in diplomatic channels in the way that he has sought to proceed, and I am certainly satisfied with your manifest qualifications to fulfill the role for which you have been nominated.

I have no further questions. We will utilize the remainder of our time for discussion with several witnesses of the second question that brings us here today; that is, in addition to considering your nomination, to hear many points of view on the general proposition of United States-Vatican relations.

Senator Pell, do you have any further questions?

Senator PELL. No further questions.

Senator LUGAR. We will excuse you from the witness table, Mr. Wilson, and call forward the additional witnesses. We thank you and the members of your family for coming.

APPENDIX III

Senate Hearing on the Nomination of Ambassador Melady

Hearing

Before the

Committee on Foreign Relations

United States Senate

on nomination of

Thomas Patrick Melady

to be

The U.S. Ambassador to the Holy See

July 19, 1989

Washington, D.C.

STATEMENT OF HON. THOMAS PATRICK MELADY, OF CONNECTICUT, TO BE AMBASSADOR TO THE HOLY SEE

Mr. Chairman, it is an honor for me to appear before the Committee as the nominee of the President to serve as the U.S. Ambassador to the Holy See.

I respect the constitutional requirement of Senatorial consent, and I am pleased to participate in the process.

It is a special privilege to be nominated to serve as U.S. Ambassador, and I deeply appreciate this manifestation of confidence in me by President Bush.

Setting forth my qualifications for this post is a humbling process. The importance of the Holy See in world affairs as a force for peace and justice assumes special significance as new opportunities evolve for the ameliorating of tensions between major political systems.

The improvement in the standard of living for peoples in developing countries, the forward movement for greater religious freedom in countries where this has not been so, and the growing worldwide commitment to end racial and ethnic discrimination present themselves as clear opportunities as we enter the last decade of this century.

After my university studies in 1955, I began my career in a developing country, where I worked in economic development matters and taught as a volunteer in the YMCA program. My subsequent career in higher education focused of Third World societies.

As a Professor of Government and International Relations, I have taught courses in U.S. foreign policy and the United Nations. Most of my research and publications have concentrated of geopolitical and economic development in Africa and Asian countries.

Since completing my assignment as a university president in 1986, I have been involved primarily in public policy matters in the State of Connecticut. As President of the Connecticut Public Expenditure Council, I directed the research and was a spokesmen for our positions on economic and governmental policy questions in Connecticut.

This service was, in many ways, a continuation of my commitment to seek better government through bipartisan efforts to use objective data in guiding public policy decisions.

Entwined throughout my careers in higher education, diplomacy, and public affairs have been some corollary activities in ecumenical, human rights, and cultural organizations. I have been especially active in organizations that nurture pluralism and citizen participation.

Mr. Chairman, I believe, I like to think, that my thirty-four years of experience, working in economic development projects, participation in international conferences in education, culture, and race relations, representing the U.S. as an Ambassador to two African countries, and as an advisor to the U.S. Delegation to the U.N., and, most recently, in designing a plan to utilize private-sector resources for training programs of Third World nationals have helped me to prepare for this new opportunity for service.

The Holy See today seeks solutions to the challenges of economic development, religious and social justice inequities, tensions between competing political systems, and the promotion of human rights.

As the ambassador of the Government of the United States, I would represent our government in presenting our point of view and seeking concurrence in these areas of convergent and parallel interest.

There is so much that can be done in this post by representing our government's policy. I would hope to play a role in our country's worldwide commitment to greater peace and prosperity for all peoples in the world.

If confirmed, Mr. Chairman, I am ready to assume this responsibility.

Thank you.

Senator Biden: Thank you.

Senator Biden: Representing the U.S. positions to the Vatican in light of the involvement, the stepped up involvement, that the Vatican has in world affairs, particularly under the tenure of Pope John Paul II, and the way the world is changing so radically, it is interesting. How do you assess the recognition of Poland after a resumption of a break of fifty years in diplomatic relations?

What impact do you see that having? Is that just parochial in that Pope

John Paul is a Pole, as the Poles have a specific domestic requirement and the pressure is on the government to do that, or do you see it as larger than that?

Ambassador Melady: I think it is larger than that, Mr. Chairman. There are those factors. The Holy Father has a Polish background, and there is the heritage, the history. That is all there. But there is a landmark, a historic landmark is an evolving situation, where we see greater religious freedom, greater emphasis on human rights and pluralism in the Eastern European countries and the Soviet Union itself.

I have been down here for the past three or four months doing my homework for the position and have been reading the very excellent background files. From this and my own reading, I knew it has been coming for some time — negotiated, discussed, certain things had to be set forth, then it happened a few days ago.

I think it is a landmark in an evolving situation. It is one of the great opportunities.

I sit here and look at you and see the map on the wall of Eastern Europe, and I think of historic changes that are taking place and that have to be monitored. I think our presence at the Holy See will help us to monitor them and to have some influence. I think it is a landmark, Senator. There were perhaps some idiosyncratic, special reasons, such as the background of the Holy Father, but it is larger than that.

Senator Biden: You have been involved over the years in our church, in the Catholic Church, as a layperson. Your volunteerism in that sector is well known, and your interest is also well known. Do you see that as an asset, as a liability, or as of no consequences in your fulfilling you role as ambassador?

Ambassador Melady: I would say as the Ambassador of the United States Government, a religious affiliation should not really have any direct part of it.

It is a fact that in my life I have been active as a lay person in pluralistic activities, in the Third World, and in religious freedom. I think that broad a perspective should be an asset to me in fulfilling the role of United States Ambassador.

Senator Biden: Obviously one of the bones of contention or points of disagreement that we have had with the Vatican is Israel and the recognition of Israel. The Holy See, although recognizing Israel's right to exist, and the Pope has met with Israeli officials on several occasions, has declined to establish full diplomatic ties, asserting that its recognition of Israel should occur only after a Middle East peace agreement that would clearly define Israel's borders and satisfy Palestinian demands for a national homeland. What are the prospects, in your view, for improved relations between the Holy See and Israel? Do you think the Vatican could play a constructive role in the effort to promote a Middle East peace settlement? Or have they just so damaged their credibility with Israel that that is not possible?

Ambassador Melady: You are right, Senator. That is one of the areas where I mentioned convergence of parallel interests lie. As the Ambassador of the United States, if I am confirmed and go there, I will express another point of view on this. We not only recognize the State of Israel, the sovereign, independent state, but we also think the Holy See should. That obviously is a place where do not do exactly converge.

I will seek to continue to present that point of view and the reasons for it.

I think, again, looking at the map, that in that area of the Middle East, some of the new opportunities, going back to President Carter's Administration, such as the Camp David Accords, were historic movements forward. Building on that and looking at some improvements in some of the neighboring areas, we can be cautiously optimistic. We know the history and the centuries of tensions, exacerbated by religious and economic differences.

We do not have any choice but to continue the dialogue and to move on. I will continue to represent our point of view to the Holy See and what we think would be done, and I would hope to have some impact.

Senator Biden: Do you think tensions are diminishing or increasing between the Vatican and Israel? There is the situation of the convent at a former death camp. There is the failure to recognize. There is the criticism of an overly ambitious embracing of a Palestinian cause and the PLO.

How do you see the situation now? Has it deteriorated in the last three to five years or has it gotten better?

Ambassador Melady: I think there are some issues here. I have been active in this field and have had some dialogue —

Senator Biden: That's why I ask.

Ambassador Melady: — with my various friends in the community, including the Jewish Community, and there are some concerns that need to be cleared up. You mentioned the convent situation in Poland. That is not directly a matter of U.S. government interest.

Senator Biden: No, it is not, but it impacts.

Ambassador Melady: It has impacted certainly. However, some of the other things you mentioned are, when it comes to the Middle East, such as the question of the relationship with the several Palestinian leaders.

There are many things. Perhaps if you read the literature in standard American and European newspapers, there are things such as the dialogue improved after the Vatican declaration on Jewish people, and so forth, and I played a role in some of those activities.

There was then a plateau, and perhaps things have taken a slight dip. We will have to work to see if we cannot correct that dip.

Senator Biden: Do you think it is important that that dip be corrected?

I guess what I am trying to get at is this. You have extensive background and are very knowledgeable about the activity and the role and the interest of the Vatican in your capacity as a layperson as well as a professional. Couple that with your knowledge of and support of U.S. positions on matters that relate. In this case to Israel. How important is it that the Vatican be perceived worldwide as being more sympathetic to the position of Israel and Jews in general?

Ambassador Melady: Senator, you will have to remember that if I go there and am confirmed, I will be the Ambassador of the United States Government.

Senator Biden: Yes, I understand that. That is what I am asking you about, from that position. The reason I prefaced the comment was to acknowledge your knowledge and background.

I could have asked similar questions to other nominees, who would not have had the background coming into the job. Maybe I should not give you as much credit as I have. So let me drop the preface.

How important is it, from the position of the United States Government, that the Vatican be perceived here and in other places as being more sympathetic to the concerns and problems facing Israel, as well as Jewish people worldwide?

Ambassador Melady: I think it is in the interest of what the Vatican, the Holy See, wants to accomplish in regard to the reduction of tensions, to have that feeling of trust and take a serious interest in reducing the tensions. It cannot be done overnight, some of these matters. But there are things that can be done. There is serious interest and doing your homework, and a real desire to move from here to here (indicating) — maybe not to there right away (indicating), but from here to here (indicating). With modern communications, instant communications, really, I am cautiously optimistic.

Senator Biden: Well, I'm frank to tell you that I have been disappointed and somewhat surprised, and not fully able to understand why some of the things that have been done, minor in the scheme of things, but seem to be adding up to increasing the tensions rather than diminishing tensions.

It is only part of the world where I get the impression the Vatican, regardless of its intentions, and I assume them to be noble, has increased, rather than diminished, tensions.

I am a little bit surprised.

I sincerely hope that in your tenure as ambassador you will be able to persuade the Vatican that a greater degree of sensitivity may be warranted. At least that has been our government's position generally. I know you would pursue our government's position vigorously.

But I think you are going to have your hands full. I wish you a great deal of luck. You will have my support, for what that is worth. But I really do not view this position, nor do you, obviously, as a throwaway. I view this as an important piece in what is going to be an extremely complicated reshaping — well, to say "reshaping" may be an exaggeration — but a complicated shift in relationships, not only in Europe and Eastern Europe, but in the Middle East, in which the Vatican can, and must, in my view, play a very positive role. By and large, it has.

I wish you luck.

You are in the dubious position, once you become ambassador, of probably having more people being interested in seeing you than you had when you were in equally important positions in two African countries. The mere fact that you will be located in Rome I am sure has nothing to do with that. But I expect you will be seeing and hearing from your colleagues in the State Department as well as your colleagues up here on the Hill.

I wish you luck and offer you the assistance of this Committee in the carrying out of your functions. I think they are important, what you are about to attempt to undertake.

Ambassador Melady: Thank you, Mr. Chairman. I look forward to working at this.

I respect this process in the Committees, and I look forward to working with you, if confirmed.

Senator Biden: Thank you very much. I don't think there is going to be much problem with that.

I again would thank your family for being gracious enough to go through their lunch hour. This means that you are going to owe them a nice lunch.

Ambassador Melady: I'll take them out to lunch.

Senator Biden: Again, thank you very, very much.

Senator Biden: I thank you all for sitting through these important hearings, and the hearings on the nominations are now closed.

(Whereupon, at 1:25 p.m., the hearing was concluded.)

APPENDIX IV
Exchange of Credentials

Exchange of credential remarks
on October 1, 1989

[Both speeches were prepared weeks in advance of the October 1, 1989, ceremony and were intended to set forth the framework of the U.S.-Holy See relationship at the beginning of the Tenure of Ambassador Melady.

The speeches were not given orally but presented at the ceremony. The Pope and Ambassador Melady then had a private discussion.]

Your Holiness:

It is a great honor to present to you my credentials as Ambassador of the United States of America to the Holy See.

Not long ago, you received President Bush in this same library. The President has told me how much he appreciated his audience with you, and how he values your counsel on international issues. I feel privileged to be able to continue, on a regular basis, my country's fruitful consultations with the Holy See, and look forward to building on the fine work of my predecessor, Ambassador Frank Shakespeare.

No one who has followed Your Holiness's travels throughout the world — including two visits to the United States, which we recall so fondly — can ignore the profound moral influence exerted by the Holy See. You have brought the Church to the world in an unprecedented way. For all of us interested in peace, justice, and human rights, the Holy See's worldwide influence is a crucial force in international diplomacy. The months since the visit of President Bush have seen additional examples of the Holy See's leadership role in seeking morally just solutions to problems caused by competing political structures.

In your 1989 address to the Diplomatic Corps here, you called for the "emergence of the concept of freedom of religion as an authentic civil and social right." As you had hoped, that notion took explicit form in the final Vienna document of the Conference on Security and Cooperation in Europe — in large part because of the skillful efforts of the Holy See delegation to the Conference. We are pleased that much of the international community has accepted the view that religious freedom is inseparable from — indeed, the foundation of — the entire range of human rights.

As we assess the remarkable changes occurring in Central and Eastern Europe today, we see that the people, if not always their governments, understand the vital connection between freedom of worship and other rights. But there is still much progress to be made. We will continue to join the Holy See in urging that, from the Baltic to the Ukraine and beyond, the principles of Vienna become everyday realities.

As we look to other regions of the world, we find reasons for hope — and cause for concern. In all of those areas, we value our discussions with the Holy See. In Central America, you have called for full compliance with the Esquipulas II accords. We agree, and on the basis of a bipartisan accord between the White House and the Congress are working to help bring peace and democratization to the region. We admire the courage and wisdom of the Church in the Central American National Reconciliation Commissions, and support their efforts. In Panama, the Bishops' Conference has set an example of bold leadership in calling for democracy.

We have taken to heart your repeated calls for peace in Lebanon, and fully share your anguish. Lebanon must not be destroyed. The Lebanese people must be free to work out their own form of government as an independent, sovereign country with territorial integrity. We are doing everything we can through diplomatic channels to bring about the disbanding of militias and the withdrawal of all foreign forces. Here again, the role of the Church is critical. The Maronite patriarch of Lebanon has worked hard to help resolve the violence and bring about presidential elections. We salute his resolve.

I have followed with enormous interest Your Holiness's five trips to

Africa. Following university studies I visited the Continent many times in preparing the materials for my books and later served in Africa as a U.S. Ambassador. I am fully aware of the important steps taken by the Holy See in the interest of peace, social justice, relief assistance, education, and reconciliation. The Vatican's recent document on racism has made an important contribution to the public debate on social structures throughout the Continent. Finally, in your visit to Madagascar, La Reunion, Zambia, and Malawi this spring, you called the world's attention — once again — to global issues such as underdevelopment, debt, and environmental pollution. As you stated in your Encyclical *Sollicitudo Rei Socialis*, these problems can only be addressed in a spirit of solidarity between richer and poorer nations.

The ethical and moral challenges inherent in the continued presence of an underclass — whether in overwhelming numbers in the developing societies or in smaller communities within the industrial nations — have been so forcefully set forth by you and your predecessor. We share these concerns.

This includes a recognition that industrial societies within their own boundaries have challenges like drug addiction and associated violence against persons. We seek the harmony among peoples so long advocated by Your Holiness and by your predecessors.

Let me conclude by returning for a moment to Europe. Last year, you addressed the European Parliament in Strasbourg and emphasized the Continent's common spiritual roots. A few days after his May 27 audience with Your Holiness, President Bush spoke of the need to reduce "artificial barriers" in Europe. Clearly, exciting changes are now taking place in East-West relations. Let us work together to encourage those changes, to the extent that they contribute to greater human rights and peace.

Your Holiness, in your May 27 remarks to President Bush, you referred to the mission of the United States "as a people engaged in good works and committed to serving others . . . as far as humanity extends." We are proud of that mission, and will continue to press for human rights and economic development for all people.

I thank you, Your Holiness, for accepting my Letters of Credence. May God grant me success in representing my government to the Holy See so that, working together, we can further the goals of peace, liberty, and justice.

Mr. Ambassador,

With great pleasure I welcome you to the Vatican and accept the Letters accrediting you as the Ambassador of the United States of America to the Holy See. It is my fervent hope that your mission will contribute to strengthening the good relations existing between the United States and the Holy See, and that the fruitful dialogue which was begun under your two predecessors will continue. I ask you to convey my cordial greetings to President Bush, assuring him and all your fellow citizens of my prayerful good wishes.

In your address, you referred to a growing conviction within the international community that religious freedom is to be recognized and protected as a fundamental human right. The Holy See has constantly proclaimed that the human person has an inalienable right to pursue the truth, to worship God and to act in accordance with the dictates of conscience (cf. *Dignitatis Humanae*, 2). This right to religious freedom must be safeguarded by the laws which govern nations. Wherever freedom of religion is denied or curtailed, human dignity itself is violated, and genuine progress toward a social order marked by justice and peace is seriously compromised.

In my recent Encyclical *Sollicitudo Rei Socialis*, I argued that the violation of fundamental human rights constitutes a kind of impoverishment as serious as any material poverty (no. 15). In this regard, I have often stressed the necessity of democratic and participatory forms of government for the growth of an orderly political life. Indeed, "the 'health' of a political community — as expressed in the free and responsible participation of all citizens in public affairs, in the rule of law, and in respect for and promotion of human rights — is the necessary condition and sure guarantee of the development of 'the whole individual and of all people' " (ibid., no. 44). Only where human freedom is fostered and protected can a social order develop which is capable of responding to the needs and aspirations of the men and women of today.

Two years ago, in the course of my second Pastoral Visit to the United States, I was pleased to recall that from the very beginning of America's history freedom has been the principle at the basis of the formation of a well-ordered society. The Constitution of the United States bears eloquent witness to your country's belief that the freedom of individuals is indispensable for the pursuit of the common good. Accordingly, the United States has come to enjoy an experience, tested by time, that a disciplined and generous freedom is the path to peace, to a just social order, and to the achievement of the good of the nation.

During my Pastoral Visit, I recall having spoken on the theme of freedom at the Ecumenical Prayer Service held in Columbia, South Carolina. On that occasion, I expressed the conviction that there can be no true freedom without moral accountability. The conquest of freedom does not lie in rejecting objective norms of conduct or in refusing to assume personal responsibility. True freedom implies that we are capable of choosing good, without constraint, and that we acknowledge our accountability for the good that we fail to do and the evil we commit. The strength or weakness of individuals and of whole societies depends on how clearly they grasp this moral imperative (September 11, 1987).

Dramatic events in recent months have drawn the world's attention to the enduring desire of entire peoples to experience the blessings of freedom and self-determination. Yet, as the lessons of your country's history have demonstrated, these blessings are often secured at great sacrifice, and may not be taken for granted from generation to generation. In every age, new challenges arise and must be confronted with confidence and resolution. The profound threat to human freedom posed by the illegal traffic in narcotics is but one example. The curse of drug addiction, which hovers like a dark cloud over entire nations, is surely one of the most serious menaces to freedom in our time.

I thank you, Mr. Ambassador, for your reference to Lebanon. The present situation in that country is of utmost concern to the Holy See, as I have repeatedly manifested in appeals and public prayers for the end of violence and for the beginning of a new era of peace and progress in that sorely tried land. The Apostolic See hopes that present and future efforts to secure the normalization of life in Lebanon will help to strengthen the unity of her people as a free and sovereign nation.

You have also drawn attention to the Holy See's work for the promotion of peace and a just social order in Africa. I am particularly pleased to note the assistance given to Africa's many developing countries as they continue to take their place within the family of nations. In calling for a spirit of solidarity with them, I am well aware of the great human resources which they have to offer to the world at large. Your own knowledge and experience of that Continent will surely confirm this judgment. I am confident that the United States will continue its generous support of these nations which are seeking development in accord with their own highest aspirations.

Mr. Ambassador, there are reasons for gratitude as we contemplate the signs of hope reflected in the present world situation. Yet many of these signs of hope are fragile and in need of wise and careful stewardship. The presence of the Holy See in the international community seeks to promote a deeper reflection on the basic spiritual truths and values involved in human life. As a nation which exercises great influence throughout the world, I pray that America will be ever sensitive to this spiritual dimension of all human activity.

While assuring you of the cooperation of the various departments of the Holy See in the fulfillment of your new mission, I express once again my abiding esteem for the people of the United States of America. May God bless you and your important work.

From the Vatican, October 3, 1989

APPENDIX V

Letter of Instructions for Ambassador Melady

[*The following letter from Secretary of State James A. Baker, III summarized instructions that had been given orally to me in August 1989 before my departure for Rome. This communication was originally classified as <u>Secret.</u> The document was released at the author's request by the U.S. Department of State.*]

THE SECRETARY OF STATE
WASHINGTON
January 17, 1990

Dear Tom:

To guide you in your role as Chief of Mission, which you assumed in August, I would like to review our essential objectives in the Holy See.

The Holy See has a global perspective. It is a significant force for human rights, and is frequently asked to help find peaceful solutions to regional disputes. Its pronouncements on major issues such as arms control, debt, and development, refugees, environment, and narcotics reach a worldwide constituency.

Relations between the Holy See and the United States cover a broad range of important concerns and are excellent. Our overall objective is to maintain and strengthen the warm ties and sense of trust between us. We in Washington will rely on you to recommend ways to further our relationship, highlighting key areas of convergence and divergence in our analyses of current events and long-term trends. We will also count on you to explain and advocate our positions.

The Holy See plays a major role in the changing configuration of Europe, especially with respect to Poland, Hungary, and the USSR. You should work to ensure that the appeal to good relations among geographical neighbors does not obscure the importance of underlying values and support for freedom. You should underscore the importance of prudence and a united Western approach.

The Holy See is concerned about the Middle East, particularly Lebanon and Occupied Territories. It seeks to improve relations between Muslim and Christian communities in the region. You should emphasize our deep commitment to finding a peaceful solution to Middle East conflicts. You should also urge the Holy See to recognize the State of Israel. In Central America, the Holy See is a force for democratic reform through its support of Cardinal Obando y Bravo in Nicaragua. You should encourage this support and also foster similar concern for democracy throughout Latin America.

In Africa, the Holy See has been involved in mediation between warring factions in Angola and Mozambique. You should maintain close contact on these disputes. The Holy See is also working in Asia to strengthen the position of religious minorities and advocate progress in human rights. You should emphasize our continuing efforts to further human rights.

SECRET

The Holy See desires major reductions in nuclear arms. You should make clear our commitment to arms control while noting the essential role of nuclear deterrence in maintaining stability and peace. You should advocate our belief that free economic systems hold out the best hope for ending poverty and provide the soundest underpinnings for free political systems and the protection of human rights. Other topics where the Holy See can play an important role are in the areas of drug trafficking and abuse, denouncing terrorism, supporting the environment, and continuing efforts to promote solutions to refugee problems.

I will touch on only the most essential points of your authority over the U.S. Mission. These are more fully expanded in the enclosed statement, which you should regard as an integral part of this letter.

— Your authority derives from the President's constitutional responsibilities for the conduct of foreign affairs and flows from him through me to you.

— The only authorized channel for instructions to you is through me or directly from the President. Assistant Secretary Seitz will issue instructions in my name and serve as the primary communications link between us.

— I am — and, by extension, you are — personally responsible for the protection of all U.S. Government personnel on official duty abroad (other than those personnel under the command of a U.S. area military commander) and their accompanying dependents.

— You have full responsibility for the direction, coordination, and supervision of all U.S. Government executive branch employees at the Holy See.

— You have full control over the size, composition, and mandate of all Mission elements, and should use your authority to reduce overall Mission size whenever possible.

— To accomplish the many tasks before you, you must directly involve yourself in the management of Mission resources, programs, and staff.

Sincerely yours,

James A. Baker, III

APPENDIX VI
Ambassador's Parting Letter

[A departing ambassador leaves a personal letter for his successor. The following was left by Ambassador Melady.]

EMBASSY OF THE

UNITED STATES OF AMERICA

TO THE HOLY SEE

Rome, Italy

March 1, 1993

Dear Fourth U.S. Ambassador to the Holy See,

As you assume your duties here I wish you every success. My almost four years as the Third U.S. Ambassador to the Holy See were great years for my wife and me. We will leave this evening with many beautiful memories.

You will find a fine staff here; the same at the residence. I have left a more detailed report with the Deputy Chief of Mission.

The Secretariat of State at the Holy See is composed of competent and dedicated men. I leave here with a high appreciation of them. We generally agreed. On a few matters we did not. They were always gentlemen and I now regard many as my friends.

Please do not hesitate to contact me whenever I can be helpful to you in your mission.

With my warmest best wishes for all God's choicest blessings, I am

Very sincerely yours,

Tom Melady

INDEX

committed to recognizing the
independence of Slovenia and Croatia,
142; most successful cooperative
diplomatic effort, 59; position on
Israel, 124; relationship should be
regarded as very serious business, 176
Human rights and religious freedom:
cornerstone of U.S.-Holy See relations
• 77-94
Humanitarian concerns • 111, 163
Hume, Cameron, U.S. Embassy Deputy
Chief of Mission • 9, 74, 81, 86, 88,
93, 134, 142
Hungary • 25, 57, 59, 69, 70, 21

I

Idi Amin: Hitler in Africa • 2, 118
Immigrants, immigration • 43, 45, 160, 170
Indonesia • 89, 90, 170
Instant communications • 13, 18, 19, 23,
160, 174, 207
Instructions • 14, 15, 19, 20, 33, 37, 95,
115, 120, 121, 124, 126, 134, 137, 140,
144, 146, 157, 165, 166, 214, 216
Interest in the arts • 172
International drug traffic • 21, 22, 28, 164,
167; I. League for Human rights 79; I.
police effort to free Kuwait • 119
Intervention in Bosnia • 146
Islamic law • 85
Israel • 13, 33, 61, 91, 109, 116, 117, 120,
121, 124-136, 205-207, 215; fall 1992:
visit of Foreign Minister Peres, 133; I.
and Arab countries talking, 132;
positive signal at a time of rising
anti-Semitism, 133; State of I. and the
Holy See, 124, 134
Italy • 14, 26, 29, 41, 43, 50, 76, 86, 92,
114, 115, 128, 133, 142, 143, 217;
Garibaldi's unification, 42; Israeli
Ambassador to I., *see* Pazner

J

John Paul II, Pope • 9, 11, 15-19, 24-29,
34-36, 38, 48, 57-61, 65, 66, 67-69, 75,
78-80, 83, 85, 89, 96-98, 106, 127,
133, 136, 141, 144, 146, 151, 152,
154-156, 158, 159, 161, 164-166, 174,
175, 189, 204; address on January 11,
1992, 27; arrival in Jakarta, 89;
attempted assassination in 1981, 73;
Centesimus Annus, Encyclical, 11, 35,

153, 154, 161, 162; collectivism
increases alienation, 159; February
1993 trip to Africa, 84; June 7, 1982,
historic meeting with President
Reagan, 59; homily in East Timor, 90;
horror of the use of war, 155; personal
message to transmit to President Bush,
121; trip to Africa, February 1993, 84;
visit to Denver, 174, 175; visit to
Lithuania, September 4-8, 1993, 65;
not pacifist at any cost, 114; sent
Archbishop Tauran to war-ravaged
Yugoslavia, 142; Slavs of Eastern
Europe in his vision of a European
community, 67; spoke of a united
Christian Europe, 58; will not be
selective in his criticism, 176
John XXIII, Pope • 35, 153; *Mater et
Magistra*, Encyclical, 153; *Pacem in
Terris*, Encyclical, 35
Joint Commission on Israel-Holy See
Relations • 132, 133
Just War teaching • 32, 46, 113, 116;
problem, fifth and sixth criteria, 114
Justice and Peace, Pontifical Council for •
89, 168, 169, 182, 212; energizer of the
worldwide Catholic network, 168

K

Karlov, Jurij, representative of Soviet
Union and Russian Federation to the
Pope • 18, 76, 116
Kennedy, John Fitzgerald, 35th U.S.
President • 51, 52
Kimmit, Robert, former U.S.
Undersecretary of State • 21
King, Rufus, last U.S. Minister to Papal
States • 42, 101
Kissinger, Henry, former U.S. Secretary of
State • 33, 75
Klenicki, Rabbi Leon • 62
Korec, Cardinal Ján C., Archbishop of
Nitra, Slovakia • 68
Kremery, Dr. Karol, Slovak leader • 68
Kuharic, Cardinal Franjo, Archbishop of
Zagreb • 142

L

Laboa, Archbishop José Sebastián, Nuncio
to Panama • 22
Laghi, Archbishop Pio, first Nuncio to the
U.S. • 60, 79

President of Tanzania • 33

O

O'Connor, Cardinal John J., Archbishop
of New York • 115, 116, 127, 128;
guest at ambassadorial residence for
luncheon, 128; meeting with Pope John
Paul II, 127; Middle East visit, 127
Opposition to Embassy status in 1984
hearings • 53
Osius, Ted, III, Embassy Political Officer •
9, 134

P

Pacelli, Eugenio • 44; *see* Pius XII, Pope
Pacem in Terris, Encyclical • 35
Palestinian rights • 125
Palmer, Andrew, British Ambassador to
the Holy See • 77
Papacy • 15-17, 21, 22, 26, 34, 35, 38,
41-44, 46, 49, 50, 53, 55, 58, 65, 75,
79, 84, 85, 95, 98, 101, 107, 121, 122,
124, 135, 141, 145, 147, 150, 153, 156,
157, 159, 161, 162, 168, 169, 174, 178,
179, 183, 184, 188, 191, 192, 193, 197;
see also Pope
Papal statements on the drug menace • 21;
P. States 41-43, 46, 49, 50, 101,
191-193, 197
Paraguay • 25, 79, 80
Paul VI, Pope • 34, 35, 100, 153; address
to the United Nations, 33, 34; calling
attention to worldwide poverty, 35;
Populorum Progressio, Encyclical, 34,
153
Pazner, Avi, Israeli Ambassador to Italy •
128-129, 133-135
Pilarczyk, Archbishop Daniel E.,
Cincinnati • 115
Pinochet Ugarte, General Augusto,
President of Chile • 80
Pius XI, Pope, *Quadragesimo Anno*,
Encyclical • 35, 153
Pius XII, Pope • 16, 44, 45, 56, 65, 139
Poland • 11, 16, 25, 26, 48, 58-61, 63,
65-67, 69, 70, 133, 155, 188, 189, 195,
200, 204, 206, 215
Polk, James Knox, 11th U.S. President •
42
Pontifical Commission for the Pastoral
Care of Migrants and Itinerant Peoples
• 170

Pontifical Council for Justice and Peace •
89, 168, 169, 182; for Pastoral
Assistance to Health Care Workers,
163, 182
Pope • 9-12, 15-19, 21, 24-28, 30, 31,
33-38, 41-50, 55-61, 63, 65, 66-69, 71,
73-75, 78-81, 83-85, 87-92, 95-100,
103, 106, 114, 116, 117, 121-123,
126-128, 133, 135-137, 139-142,
144-146, 149, 151, 152, 153-170,
174-176, 178, 179, 188, 189, 195, 200,
201, 204, 205, 209; moral power, 165;
right to speak should be protected, 176;
role, 44, 45, 159, 161, 179; role as an
authoritative voice, 161; *see* also
Papacy, individual Popes
Populorum Progressio, Encyclical • 34,
153
Position of the Holy See on Israel • 124
Positive signal needed at a time of rising
anti-Semitism • 133
Problem: the fifth and sixth [Just-War]
criteria • 114

Q

Qaddafi, Muammar Muhammad al-,
Libyan leader • 36, 131
Quadragesimo Anno, Encyclical • 35, 153
Quayle, Marilyn, wife of former Vice
President • 85

R

Randell, Alexander W., U.S. Diplomatic
Representative to Papal States • 42, 101
Raphael I Bidawid, Patriarch of the
Chaldean Church of Iraq • 119
Re, Archbishop Giovanni Battista, Vatican
Substitute Secretary of State • 128
Reagan, Ronald Wilson, 40th U.S.
President • 24, 31, 41, 48-53, 58-61,
74, 153-155, 174, 175, 192; meeting
with Pope John Paul II, 59
Recognition • 29, 41-46, 50, 51, 53, 64,
109, 124, 126, 131, 136, 141-144, 149,
178, 204, 205, 211
Redistribution of the world's resources •
37, 169, 170
Refugees • 12, 56, 69, 81, 85, 170, 172,
178, 215
Rerum Novarum, Encyclical • 35, 153
Rights of Palestinian people • 125
Robu, Iaon, Archbishop of Budapest • 72